Roots of England

ROOTS of ENGLAND

JOHN MILLER & SID WADDELL

British Broadcasting Corporation

Authors' Note

As with the films, so with this book, our thanks are due to the many academics, librarians, local historians, both professional and amateur, journalists and broadcasting colleagues who have contributed their thoughts to our researches. Most of all, though, our thanks must go to the English families, communities and individuals, those mentioned in the book, and many who are not, whose lives we set out to examine and reflect. We are happy to report that the English, in all their guises, are still a helpful, hospitable race!

John Miller
Sid Waddell

Published by the
British Broadcasting Corporation
35 Marylebone High Street
London W1M 4AA

ISBN 0 563 17792 6

First published 1980

© British Broadcasting Corporation 1980

Printed in England
by Jolly & Barber Ltd, Rugby

Contents

Introduction

Recent years have seen an upsurge in national awareness all around England's borders – Scots, Welsh and Irish each claiming a 'special identity' separate from the rest of Great Britain. But what of the English? On their side of the borders too there is a growing awareness that the English are different – not only from those other nations but within their own – and that the differences are worth preserving.

Three years ago the authors of this book set out to look at some of those differences. Cheek by jowl with the anonymous high streets, the grey industrial estates and the 'factory' farms they found pockets, whole patches, of an older England every bit as varied as Daniel Defoe, Celia Fiennes, William Cobbett or J. B. Priestley found on their respective journeys. It is true that local customs and traditions are being eroded by many different forces, yet at the same time there is a growing awareness of the value of what is under attack. The sprouting of local museums, of environmental, historical and dialect societies shows that there is now a positive determination to save the variety of the English heritage.

This book, and the films on which it is based, is an attempt to reflect twelve English localities through the people who know them best – the people who live there. To get hold of the essence of a place, though, is a dangerously ambitious undertaking. One person's way of seeing things can be quite different from another's, and if you have passed through or once lived in – or even *now* live in – any of the places this book explores, you may find that their image here does not tally with your own. What is very clear, though, is that you couldn't confuse any one of them with any other – and if the films and the book had been about twenty-four places – or forty-eight – that would still hold true.

England is infinitely variable and that goes for the people who live in it, too. I think I really became aware of that first when I was working on a Radio 4 magazine programme called 'Talkabout'. Six times a year the programme came as an outside broadcast from one of the further-flung outposts of the North Region. At that time I was being paid to look at and talk about the characteristics of England, which seemed to give me a professionally-sharpened awareness of the look and feel of places that I would not have had as a mere tourist.

So I began to notice, as I hadn't before, that the fences in Lincolnshire are not the same as the fences in Lancashire; that the architectural 'feel' of a village in Cheshire is very different from one in Northumbria; that the shape of the hills and the kind of tree and even the colour of green fields can change altogether within a couple of miles – and all those differences that I was seeing were just within one region. 'Roots of England', of course, spreads its net much wider. From, for instance, a tin-mining village in Cornwall to a coal-mining village in Northumbria and, inevitably, the differences are much more marked. So marked, in fact, that it puts the idea of England – let alone Britain – as an homogeneous nation under some considerable strain. Administratively it is; but administrative convenience is not the same as popular belief. Local government boundaries say that the wool town of Saddleworth is in Greater Manchester. For all that, boys born there qualify to play for the Yorkshire Cricket Team and the locals still regard themselves as Yorkshiremen. That identifies the strength of their sense of place – and the fact that I regard their unwillingness to become adoptive sons of either Manchester or Lancashire as stubborn folly identifies mine!

Even though I grew up with that particular conviction – or prejudice – it was still a shock to hear the people of St Just-in-Penwith talk about 'the English' as if they were a different race from a different land. 'Well,' they said, 'they are – and it is.' Nor did they say it with any degree of affectation; it's taken – and stated – as a matter of fact.

On occasion, the difference sounds even more marked than it may in fact be, and the local accents which speak for themselves add considerably to the enjoyment of the films.

One of the people I talked to for the Ashington film was the General Secretary of the Northumbrian Miners' Union. Once a pit-face worker, these days, for the most part, he lives behind a desk or the wheel of a car. I asked him how he managed to keep fit now that his work no longer demands hard physical effort.

'Well,' he said, 'Ah gau ta the Torkish Baths twice a week – an' Ah have the Durg.'

I asked him if that was some kind of Oriental massage.

'Eh, son? What's that?'

'The Durg,' I said. 'Is it some kind of Oriental massage?'

He looked puzzled – not to say suspicious. There was a less than comfortable pause. Then he said: 'The durg's what Ah tak for a waak every night, man!'

In the embarrassment of the moment, I missed the dog's name . . .

Confusing, contradictory, welcoming, resentful, it's the people that make and are also made by the locale.

Certainly, places without people are pretty sterile, and places rather than people are what the tourist sees. Yet places and people are so intricately interwoven that it's almost impossible to separate them. It's a sort of folk cliché to say that people are all the same but I think that's only true at the most basic level. It's true enough that if you talk to a Northumbrian Labour Councillor about local politics, to a Suffolk farmer about agrarian policy, to a Midlands industrialist about man-management relations, then they're going to sound pretty much the same as their counterparts from other areas of England. But it's also true that people are shaped by their environment and their experiences and since you can see just by looking that environments can differ enormously, since no two people go through the same set of experiences, it's obviously inevitable that there will be that infinite variety of individuals which is what makes our working life, our choice of partners and our television programmes worth-while.

There are threats to the continuing richness of this variety: the growing number of holiday houses in the traditional enclaves of farming and fishing are forcing the native population into the towns from which the holidaymakers are escaping. Another irony is that the media make us more aware of other people's ways, other people's standards and a too frequent anxiety to conform does the rest.

Like the whale, what the authors of this book call 'The English Difference' is threatened. Like the whale, it's worth saving. I hope this book helps to do that.

Brian Trueman
Presenter of the television film series

The Black Country

Oh the chainmaker lad he's a masher,
He's always a-smoking his pipe,
He's always a-whistling the wenches,
Especially on Saturday night . . .

That Black Country traditional song, as remembered by Lucy
Woodall who spent fifty-five years making chain by hand, points to
the chainmaker as every local lass's hero. Although the trade is now
largely a thing of the past, the swagger of self-confidence implied in
the song is still central to the Black Countryman's pride in independence and in what he sees as his separate identity.

So whatever else the outsider does, he should never confuse the
Black Country with Birmingham, or he will not be forgiven. Precise
definition on the other hand is difficult. Black Countrymen will argue
with residents of West Bromwich, Stourbridge and even Wolverhampton about their eligibility for membership, but somewhere in the
middle of these three, with its centre in Dudley eight miles to the west
of Birmingham, is the collection of urban 'villages' that with a fierce
pride the locals call the 'Black Country'.

Not that Dudley is the 'capital' even then, any more than Tipton or
Coseley, Cradley Heath or Netherton. Local rivalries are constantly
kept warm as if with the metalworker's bellows. No sooner has any
Black Countryman finished defining to you his version of what
comprises the area, than he'll be telling you, with scarcely pause for
breath, about the exceptional qualities of his particular bit of it.

Perhaps in the end the area is best defined by its geography and
geology, although its mineral deposits of coal, iron ore and limestone
are now worked out. Until comparatively recent times the area was a
remote plateau with only one road running across it. Then, quite
suddenly, it was opened up by canals at the beginning of the Industrial Revolution, canals built to transport the coal from the magni-
ficent thirty-foot seam that lay beneath the plateau. It is this coal that
is generally thought to have given the area its name.

Turner painted the Dudley scene around 1832, and this engraving from it was made for a contemporary travel book

Dividing the plateau in two are the Rowley Hills, source of the 'Rowley Rag', a sombre black stone used years ago to pave the streets of Birmingham and to furnish many a dismal churchyard. The hills run from south-east towards the north-west, with Dudley Castle perched high in the middle. To the north the land is flatter, the world of work much more cosmopolitan. This is the land of the big metal trades, mass producers of identical components for customers such as the motor industry of Coventry and Birmingham to the east. Today these factories supply in bulk what local skills once produced piecemeal. If you want nuts and bolts and locks by the ton, go north, but if you want a clearer idea of the craftsmen that made the Black Country character, the evidence is stronger in the other direction.

It is to the south of Dudley Castle along the winding grey roads that to the outsider appear to go nowhere, that you will find, among the sprawl of pubs and houses, the dozens of small metal-working enterprises that are the legacy of the Black Country's past.

Opposite the Spring Meadow House pub in Cradley Heath is a narrow cobbled alley leading to the tin-roofed collection of buildings where the Bradneys, father and son, still carry on one of the last of

Britain's cottage industries, the hand-making of chain 'at the fire'. Even fifty or sixty years ago, most of the houses had a backyard 'hearth' for making chain or nails. Nailmaking by hand, more often woman's work than men's, died out with mechanisation long ago, but although today's machine-made mild-steel chain has largely replaced the hand-made wrought iron, there is still a living to be made for short runs and odd shapes, where to set up a machine could never be economical.

Arthur Bradney, now over sixty, and thirty-year-old Michael, obviously thrive on this kind of individuality. One specialist job recently was the reworking of decorative chains for Cardiff Castle, but apart from chain their 'odd-work' includes meat hooks, conveyor hooks for the motor industry, rope hooks, pulleys, anchor bolts and hatch dogs for trawlers, eye bolts, and U-bolts, scaffolding spanners and links, and tethering bars for livestock. Whether it is brackets for Bangladesh or grab-handles for the Dudley sewer, the Bradneys still have scope for satisfaction in their work.

It is obvious that Arthur Bradney takes great pride in the skill he has handed down to his son. As we filmed Michael's easy rhythm at the anvil, heating bars in the fire, bending, hammering, flicking the ribbon of red-hot chain about like a ring of paper clips, his father just stood and watched. Michael's sturdy fore-arm is tattooed with a headstone in the shape of a cross bearing the legend *In memory of Elvis*. Below his trousers there's a flash of white sock as his old pair of blue suede shoes works the treadle of the tommy hammer. It jarred somehow to be brought back to an era much nearer the present.

As Michael worked, Arthur recalled how his father initiated him into the trade: 'When I started making chain they didn't teach you, they knocked it into you. If you did a blow wrong, you got one across the wrist with a hammer shaft or anything they could pick up. They'd pull you out of the standing and show you how to make it. Then you'd get back in and try it again.'

Later, two powerful thirsts are slaked down at 'The Bull Terrier', Arthur in a smart tweed sports jacket and Michael in his purple drape suit. As they pause for breath half-way down the third pint, they express little bitterness about the past. Present pleasures to soften the hardships have always been an aim in life around here.

Even for those with years enough to remember the really hard times, memory plays tricks with the past, softens the edges of the

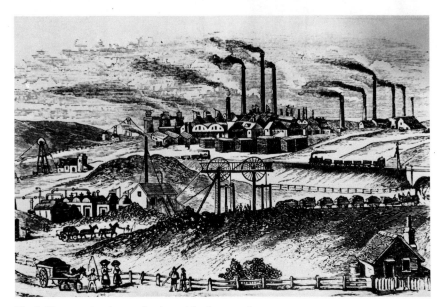
Black Country landscape in the mid-nineteenth century

bleakest thoughts. Just around the corner from the Bradney's work-shop we found Lucy Woodall, who at seventy-five had retired seven years before – the last of the lady chainmakers. She sat by the open fire of her kitchen, kettle on the hob, enamel tea-pot on the table. Crumpled hands on her lap, Lucy continued the song about the 'Chainmaker Lad', one of the many she learned when she started 'at the fire' at the age of thirteen:

> . . . Saturday night is my delight,
> Sunday morning too,
> Monday morning go to school,
> He's always after me.
> But collier boys, collier boys,
> Collier boys come in,
> Down the road, black as coal,
> And that's the chap for me.

And Lucy did eventually marry a miner!

A widow, Lucy lived with her brother-in-law who helped her get around the house on her walking frame. Her legs were in a poor way; a direct result of contact with the fire and water that are elemental to the environment of every hot-metal worker. But still her hands were

Inside a chainshop, probably Cradley Heath, in 1910. Women formed a large proportion of the workforce

strong enough to pull from a cupboard a length of fine-linked chain and show it off with pride. Each link was double and with a half-twist. Like a Chinese puzzle it was difficult to see how it was made.

She reminisced almost wistfully: 'My mother was a nailmaker. But 'er couldn't do it after 'er was married for the simple reason there wasn't a hearth where she lived. Most of the nailmakers them days had got a hearth in their own wash-house. I left school on the Friday I was thirteen and started work on the Monday at the fire. We had to serve two years' apprenticeship. We had four shilling a week for the first six months, then I had five shillings and sixpence for the next six months . . . after the two years was up you had to go on to piece-work unless it was something that couldn't be done on piece-work lines. Like lion-trap chains. I've done hundreds of lion-trap chains . . .' Yes, for catching lions!

We asked if it wasn't a bit unfair to expect girls of thirteen to work in those conditions. 'Well, there wasn't much else for girls unless they went to service, and most girls would rather work on the fire than go out to service.' The assumption that *everyone*, boy or girl, had to work was already inbred. Lucy, the last of her kind, died in October 1979.

There are still women employed in chainmaking today but most of them tend the welding machines or finish the chains with files. But in 1908 in the Cradley Heath area alone there were twelve hundred women who actually made chain. In that year their poor pay and conditions were attacked by Robert Sherard in a tract entitled *The White Slaves of England*.

Ghosts of the past crop up everywhere you go around this area, where the hills belie the title 'Black Country'. Their soft rounded shapes are as green as any in the land, but they are pocked and scarred where the underlying limestone was ripped out for iron smelting. Even the bear pits of Dudley Zoo below the castle were fashioned from the hollows left by limestone quarrying. Iron smelting disappeared with the end of the coal, but gaunt monuments to the past still stand, like Old Hawne Colliery where in the old engine house the winding wheel still hangs from rotting timbers, high above the tall, round-arched windows. Turn off any main road in Old Hill or Quarry Bank (pronounce it 'Bonk' if you ask for directions!) and you'll come across the semi-derelict premises of numerous backyard chain-shops. Behind Harry Bloomer's back gate which still bears the sign: *H. Bloomer Ltd., Registered office – Beware of the dog*, is a collection of ten chainmakers' hearths, their brick chimneys disappearing through the corrugated iron roof. But there is little smoke and fire about these days. Harry, and one young lad, potter about waiting for the big manufacturers to send down odd lengths of chain for testing on apparatus set up at the other end of the yard.

Even many of the bigger chainmaking works that grew fat in the late nineteenth century have gone downhill. Once sheds of firms like Noah Hingleys rang to the noise of men working three to a link; days when teams of horses were needed to drag away mountains of ships' chain and the anchors that went with it. Around Netherton they still remember the proud, if macabre, boast that Netherton men made the only bit of the *Titanic* that did its job – the anchor!

There are still men who work for the big firms in the old way – men like Clarry Johnson, mild and gentle in manner but a veritable Thor as he stands in a draughty shed at Barzillai Hingleys making the biggest size of chain a single man can handle, his vest a sieve of spark burns. But perhaps pagan imagery should only be applied to the workers; the bosses clearly chose their names from the Old Testament! It was a hard life, but one that has generated a lot of local pride,

Clarry Johnson and a local schoolboy making chain at Mushroom Green museum

so on the first Sunday of every month Clarry opens up the chain-shop at Mushroom Green, once a hamlet focused on a busy chain-shop, now a small industrial museum. He gets the bellows going and gives visitors a whiff of the coke fumes and a taste of the grit that was once the universal flavour of the Black Country. The flourishing Black Country Museum has rebuilt this traditional chain-shop in a conservation area where even the new houses have been built in traditional 'shoe-box' style. School parties too are brought to watch Clarry make chain at Mushroom Green. Even at twelve and thirteen they are encouraged to have a go, to take an interest in exactly how their grandfathers and grandmothers worked.

Sixth formers at Earls High School, Halesowen, were encouraged to put together a project on Mushroom Green. They produced a brochure which won a *Sunday Times* competition, but finished up themselves with a far from rose-coloured view of their past. One girl said that the inhabitants she had talked to in Mushroom Green mostly tended to look back with a sort of pride about working in the chain-shop at the age of ten, whereas she did not think it was anything to be proud of. And of loyalty to the area and its memories, another said she felt loyalty to her parents and family, but not so much to the place itself. The roots are strong in personal terms, but nobody has much to say for the physical environment or the tradition of hard work.

In getting to be one of the workshops of the world, the Black Country had to give up any pretence to elegance and sophistication. It is still not a visually attractive place by any stretch of the imagination, yet many of the present younger generation do return after college or jobs away, often to live in smart new Georgian-style semis which spring up in odd spaces between the old workshops – blobs of colour on a drab palette. Hard times and poverty were always relative here, there were far worse places. There is no tradition of boom and slump in the Black Country, no memory of dire hunger as there is in Jarrow, or of industrial strikes as in the valleys of South Wales. There was always another trade similar to your own if things went wrong. Locals will tell you proudly that the Black Country is an area that has never needed nor had any government aid; and that is a pride which is reflected in their cocky attitude to the world.

One of the most articulate exponents of Black Country philosophy is Dr John Fletcher, President of the extremely vigorous Black Country Society. Son of a factory labourer, he went to Oxford and has now returned to teach in the Modern Languages Department of Aston University, a job that allows him once again to live in the Black Country.

He sees his own progress through life as an example of a general principle. It is important to realise, he says, that in the Black Country children who get further education in a university or college can come back to the area and get jobs there. Because the people have skills that are usable in other metal trades, the Black Country has had a tradition of prosperity, despite the decline in nail and chain. If the chain industry collapsed you moved into something else. These factors have meant that in the Black Country the division between one class of society and another – manager and worker, or supervisor and worker – has not been too pronounced. As a whole the younger, fairly active, people who are attracted into the region are soon affected by the strong Black Country culture, and within a few years are almost as much Black Countrymen as the locals.

Asked whether the insistence on a strong local culture is an expression of an identity crisis, John Fletcher will tend to agree. He feels that the Black Country, unlike most industrial regions, grew up not from one centre expanding outwards but as a collection of very individual and often very isolated industrial villages; a man's first loyalty was to his own community, or even to a small part of that community. In the twentieth century the people had to face the growth of outside pressure on the area, so today Black Country people are searching for a wider loyalty, a Black Country identity, and this they are trying to create with things like the Black Country Museum, the Black Country Society, the *Black Country Bugle* (a monthly newspaper), in fact anything that uses the words 'Black Country'.

Take the 'Black Country Night Out', an attraction put on in pubs and clubs by a popular collection of local entertainers. Organised by Jon Raven, folksinger, songwriter, author and publisher, the party that regularly takes the stage are Jon himself, Brian Clift, who also writes some of his own songs, Tommy Munden, an earthy comedian who laughs *before* his own jokes, Dolly Allen, a deadpan Old Mother Riley figure who brings the house down with working-class tales of hard times, and Harry Harrison, a homespun dialect poet who also compères the shows.

On an otherwise typical night at the Citizen's Theatre behind the 'Robin Hood', Brierley Hill, they are joined by Aynuck and Ayli (Enoch and Eli), traditional Black Country characters played on this occasion by Alan Smith and John Guest. Aynuck, flat-capped and crafty, reminds Ayli, flat-capped and thick, of the time they stood in a bus queue behind a man with a glass eye. A double-decker pulled up, the man took his eye out and bounced it. It went up in the air, he caught it and put it back. What did he think he was doing, Enoch demanded, to which the man replied he was only trying to see if there was any room upstairs!

The laughter rattles the pint pots crammed on every table. The jokes are earthy but not blue, certainly not subtle, more an accurate representation of a rough, down-to-earth life. They've heard all the jokes before, but hearing them again is an excuse to laugh, not just with other people, but with other Black Country people. As you watch the faces of Clarry Johnson, Lucy Woodall, Arthur and Michael Bradney and many others like them in the audience, it is easy to see how the hearty laughter that follows each joke reflects how hard and physical the other side of life is here.

Comradeship is rough and tough, but belonging is vital. Brian Clift, born in Netherton, comes on to sing 'The Cradley Heath Song' written in recent years by his old friend Woodie Woodall. The audience knows the chorus already.

> Pin back your ears and I'll sing you a song
> Of a town that is dear to my heart,
> Where they make chains and nails, and they hold
> > jumble sales
> And everyone's mad about darts.

> *Chorus:*
> So take me back where the smoke rolls black
> And the Delph Prize Ale flows free
> Where factory wenches line all the park benches
> Cradley Heath means home to me.

> As you walk down each street friendly blokes you
> > will meet
> Their faces all full of good cheer
> But their friendship you'll doubt, when the boozers
> > turn out
> And you feel a big fist in your ear . . .

The applause is followed by long pulls on pints, and at the end of the act they are three deep at the bar which, in the Citizens' Theatre, is longer than the stage. Heavy drinking, and more especially its results, are a significant part of Dolly Allen's domestic narrative. Clutching her handbag with both hands, ostrich feather bobbing in her straw-brimmed hat, she tells of her 'man' coming home from the pub somewhat the worse for wear. Again the audience laughs readily. The image of the breadwinner letting down his hair is familiar but, as with so much of the Black Country experience, it's also a fact of life. It doesn't need Karl Marx to stress the brutalisation of repetitive heavy work. The 'gin palace' mentality is still there, but today the pubs are civilised. The booze still flows of course, but social clubs with activities of all kinds, including the Black Country Society itself, increasingly use the pubs as centres. They fill the same role as working-men's clubs in Durham or South Yorkshire.

Like most other things in the Black Country, the pubs are functional, and nearly all built to the same design, two bay windows and a central door; or seen from the inside, two window seats to get your back into, and a way out at closing time. If there is a lounge, it will generally be used for such 'official' functions as the pigeon, whippet or bull terrier society meetings, and as often as not the women will drink

'Two window seats to get your back into' – Mrs Pardoe's 'Old Swan' at Netherton

in the bar with the men. Here, too, there is little class distinction. The pubs were, and to some extent still are, there to satisfy the thirsts of men with hot and heavy work, and to provide an escape for people oppressed by a dreary life and environment. 'Real ale' is nothing new in the Black Country, which has four or five local breweries producing traditional beers, and where Mrs Pardoe's Swan Inn and Brewery at Netherton is another Black Country backyard industry. Chainmakers could always tell the difference between the real thing and the 'Burton's Returns' that were sometimes foisted on them, but in hard times they would force even that down.

Of course there were those who disapproved of drinking. Within shouting distance of every pub was a chapel, making the pub a sitting duck for the hell-fire preacher next door. Cliff Willetts, twenty-five years a striker in a chain-shop, is still a local councillor and lay preacher at eighty-three. He remembers his own mother in trouble from just such a hot gospeller: 'At our own chapel one Sunday night the preacher was laying it on that drink was the cause of all poverty, and my mother stood up in the service and said "You can say what you've a mind but I'm going to have my half pint because I think it does me good". And he said, "Carrie, you'll go to hell". Now that was the extreme. They made the fundamental mistake of saying you'd go to hell if you had half a pint of beer. But although my mother couldn't read or write, her reply was classic: "I don't care whether I go up there or down there, I shall see somebody I know!"'

Cliff's mother began work at the age of eight as a blower operating the bellows in a chain shop, and by the time she was ten was making chain herself. She worked from eight in the morning until eight at night, and on the day she got married, until nine o'clock to make up for the hour she'd taken off to walk up to the church, get married, and walk back.

Cliff believes firmly that individual character is what civilised the harsh society based on the mine or the chain shop, and made survival possible: 'My mother was typical. She got up in the morning and went to work in the chain shop for an hour and a half. Then she'd get us four lads off to school, do the washing in the 'brewus' [brewhouse, or washhouse] with just a maiding tub and dolly, then, more by way of a rest than anything, she'd do the baking There was poverty, but people like my mother fought it – and lived to be eighty-six!

The chapel where Cliff's mother had her exchange with the preacher is part of the Two Gates Ragged School where Cliff is still Sunday School Superintendent. Today, few of the Ragged Schools founded some two hundred years ago by John Pound in Portsmouth are left. Now it is the state rather than the chapel that defends children from the hurts of poverty, but to the kids who pack the Two Gates school every Sunday, the tradition of Sunday School is obviously still a warm and protective one.

Though they were by no means all religious, and as often as not on piece-work, according to Cliff Willetts no chainmaker would ever work on Sunday. In spite of this, it was on Sundays that they revealed their subservience to the masters. To Cliff, with his strong streak of independence, it was clearly a source of deep embarrassment. 'I have actually seen people when I used to go down to my granny's on a Sunday morning early, seen the women in their white pinafores, chainmakers' wives and the chainmakers themselves outside the chapel, watching the bosses passing on their way to the Wesleyans and the Parish Church, bow their heads in homage to them and say: "Good morning, master; morning master."' Cliff shook his head. 'I was sometimes disgusted by the mentality of my own class. When I used to walk down a place called Little Hill in Cradley, it said on a slate: "God bless our boss and his relations, and keep us in our proper stations!" They had the opinion the employer was responsible for their living, he created the trade and if he didn't exist, they would be without a job.'

Even the Chainmaker's Union which finally closed down in 1978 (significantly perhaps it was located in a quiet suburban semi) appears to have been for much of its life a tool of the bosses. In its one hundred years of existence it never had a strike, and at one time was used by the bosses to implement their own closed shop policies.

But those sorts of bosses are no longer in evidence, and their successors are probably young sons of the Black Country who have been away to college and come back to the relative prosperity the area has always offered. There is probably a sprinkling of them too in Harry Harrison's audience at the Black Country Night Out as he slips almost imperceptibly from his compère's gags into one of his own nostalgic folk poems that echoes the search for an identity:

> 'Abaht 'ow we spake is in the news
> Ah bet yo've 'eared all sorts uv views
> now sum reckun we accent's due ter the grime
> which goz dahn we wazzins [throats] moost uv the time
> a lot cor weigh up the way we torkin
> just keep yer ears open wen yoh walk in
> any plerce wi' Black Country folk in
> y'ole 'ear these words un Ah bay jokin' . . .

> We don't say 'do not' we just say 'doh'
> that's the truth but perhaps you know
> going is gooin' un come is cum
> if you're going home yo'me gooin' wum
> 'wheer yer bin'? is 'where have you been'?
> I trust you're with it and see what I mean
> ar' it's easy aer'kid ter gerrin a mess
> cus it ay simple yoh must confess

> Don't give in . . . that's doh gi' way
> there's just a bit more I'de like to say
> about words that we use every day
> just yewze yer yeds that's the kay

teachers at school am taychers at schewl
study a bit, we doh uz a rewl
prewve it yerself yoh tek a vote
we doh spake Inglish the way it's wrote . . .

. . . So, doh get flummoxed . . . that's simply confused
I've quoted but few of our words that are used
with accentuation there are positively more
we either wull, we woh, we shor or we cor
just get out and about listen and see
I'le hazard a guess then most will agree
aer'kid it wud be a real cryin' sherm
if Black Country folks did all spake the serm!'

The language of the Black Country, as John Fletcher explained, comes from an overlay of Saxon on Celt. As the Saxons invaded the country they drove the Celt before them into the Welsh hills, as well as up on to the plateau that is now the Black Country, beyond the navigable head of the River Severn. They overlaid the Celtic civilisation with their own civilisation, and their own language. 'You get names like Wotansburg, Wotan's fortress, now known as Wednesbury, that show how the pagan religion held on in the Black Country whereas in other parts of the country Christianity was removing those sorts of names. Some people would argue the Black Country people never had any Christianity at all! There is not much around that is Norman, apart from Dudley Castle, and throughout the Middle Ages the area was never really very prosperous. The soil was heavy and clayey; today we call it "tocky bonk". The big change came with the Industrial Revolution and the mining of coal and iron. The people became introverted and didn't accept outsiders easily, so apart from the Irish in the nineteenth century and some Asians in the recent past there have been no more general incursions into the area.'

It would, however, be a mistake to imagine that, because of the relative insularity of the Black Country, local people should be able to trace their roots back through many generations. These were mainly working people who didn't bother too much with registering births and deaths, or for that matter, in many cases, about getting married. Some families have verbal records of their relations back to about 1850, but written records are few. Cliff Willetts, for example, hasn't so much as a photograph of his own parents.

Staffordshire bull terriers and their owners

Personal roots may be difficult to trace but there is still very much a recognisable Black Country type physically. John Fletcher, with his red beard and ambling gait, described himself well: 'In stature we're Celtic, squat, well-built. They say that people in the Black Country look like Staffordshire bull terriers when they get down on all fours.' And any six-foot outsider can see the type for himself as he looks over most heads in Dudley market place.

In case anyone should doubt the comparison with the bull terrier, a visit to a meet of the Staffordshire Bull Terrier Society at the Lamp Tavern in Dudley will soon prove the point. The Staffordshire is a cross between bulldog and bull terrier, but since the 1930s a recognised breed of the Kennel Club. Though they will lick your hand and are one of the softest breeds with children, the racket in the pub if owners let two of them get their noses too close together, leaves no one in any doubt that these were originally bred as fighting dogs. Once begun, it takes some time to reduce the uproar to a background of wet snarls and snorts.

John Fletcher, known in this company not without a trace of banter as 'Dr John', brought along his own dog and, being from the 'other half' of the Black Country, soon provoked a discussion on where the best dogs come from. Not so long ago the men, no less than the dogs, would have fought over such an issue, but on that night John Fletcher's feelings of a collective identity were reflected by one of the breeders when he said: 'Probably years ago different types of dog came from different areas, but today if you've got a good dog over here, people in Darlaston will come and use him. And if there's a good dog in Darlaston, people from here will go and use that dog.'

The Black Country experience is becoming more collective, and so is the pride. Roy Phillips, the Lamp's landlord, adds: 'You know, I think this dog is a reflection of the Black Countryman himself, hard-working, hard-fighting, hard-drinking. They're bloody hard, they'll lick anything on four legs, pound for pound. Yes, a reflection of the Black Countryman himself.' They all look down with pride to the dogs tucked under the benches between their legs.

There is more local pride on display in the shadow of Dudley Castle where they are rescuing and rebuilding the past to construct an open-air museum, a Black Country museum. Chain-shops, chapels, pubs and cottages, are being taken down brick by brick and re-erected on a site once occupied by limestone kilns and a sewage treatment plant. The aim is to reconstruct on one site the entire Black Country experience of pride in making things.

It is the human capital though, the investment of years of sweat, that clearly gives most grounds for proper pride. As Cliff Willetts says: 'You don't see a man walk out of British Leyland and look at a car and say, "I made that", but you do with a chainmaker. He'd look up and down a piece of chain with pride and say, "Yes, I made that."'

Saddleworth

'There was a time when you'd have found half a dozen boxes of Havana cigars parked over there and a big Jaguar in the drive, but not now. Those days have gone . . .'

On Monday 8 October 1979 the family woollen mill of J. F. & C. Kenworthy Ltd. told their one hundred workers that they would have to close down after over a hundred and twenty-five years of manufacturing woollen textiles. In a community of twenty-one thousand the loss of a hundred jobs makes big waves, but few reactions omitted a sympathetic word for John Kenworthy senior, the firm's chairman, who had spent fifty-five years in the mill. The next day's front page report in the *Oldham Chronicle* quoted Peter Bradbury, managing director of the rival family mill along the street: 'It is very sad. Even though they are competitors, we have all been friends.'

Before Kenworthys were forced to give up the struggle, four of the five woollen mills in Saddleworth were still owned by local families, and although today with the gradual decline of the textile trade few of Saddleworth's seventy industrial units are connected with the manufacture of cloth, textiles remain the biggest single employer. So it seems appropriate that when a 'Saddleworth at Work' exhibition was organised to coincide with the four-yearly Arts Festival, pride of place at the centre of the hall should still have gone to the woollens. All the week the steady flow of local visitors showed a great deal of interest in the display of woollens, which was perhaps hardly surprising since the majority of them would have at least some first-hand experience of the mills.

Saddleworth's immediately obvious sense of community is assertive and at the same time defensive. The air of confidence is most probably based on the high proportion of its workers who have always been skilled, and this remains true in the numbers of small industrial units that have sprung up in and around the former mills. Unemployment too is relatively low, though percentage figures may be distorted by the recent emergence of the area as a fashionable address for

The Saddleworth landscape at Uppermill. Bradbury's Alexandra Mill is in the foreground, right; behind it the new housing estates are spreading up the hillsides

professional people, who mainly work elsewhere. By contrast, the need for a self-protective attitude, like the presence of the textile industry itself, is a direct result of Saddleworth's geographical position.

Little over twelve miles from the centre of Manchester, the whole district is backed up into the folds and steep valleys of the Pennines. One long section of its boundary runs across bleak moors at well over five hundred metres above sea-level. 'Saddleworth's independent spirit is pressed against the hills,' is the expression used by Lord Rhodes of Saddleworth, a life peer on the strength of his services to the community. Saddleworth was a wool enclave to the West of the Pennines long before cotton came to Lancashire. The area known as Friarmere (now part of Delph) is believed to have been given to the Cistercians of Roche Abbey in the thirteenth century. They were a pastoral order who lived by the sweat of their own brows rather than taking tithes or revenues, and though it is more likely they kept cattle

The main road through Delph

than sheep, they may well have begun the small-scale spinning and weaving of wool imported into the area to supplement the poor living to be made from agriculture in such a bleak landscape.

Referred to in Domesday Book as Wyck, the area is described as 'unvalued wasteland'. There appear to have been few developments apart from farming before the mid-eighteenth century, and certainly there was no wool boom here in the fourteenth century such as lined the pockets of landowners in the lusher lands of Gloucestershire and Suffolk. Few buildings in Saddleworth today date back before the 1750s, but once the woollen industry took off, a building boom began. The collection of small villages – Uppermill, Diggle, Dobcross, Delph, Denshaw, Greenfield, Friezland, Grasscroft, Lydgate, Scout Head, Austerlands, Grotton, Springhead – which make up Saddleworth began to grow in earnest, still well ahead of cotton's heyday in Lancashire.

So from the very beginning of its real development, Saddleworth always had more in common with Yorkshire over the hill than Manchester across the plain, and until local government re-organisation in 1974 was still an urban district within the West Riding. Naturally enough the proposal to compound the marginal insult of an Oldham, Lancs. postal address with administrative inclusion within Greater Manchester, generated considerable heat. The argument though was as much to do with independence as with continuing the Wars of the Roses, since Saddleworth's physical separation from the rest of Yorkshire across the Pennines had meant the development of a community that was both self-contained, self-reliant, and therefore, above all, anti-bureaucracy.

Lord Rhodes recalled attending a local meeting which voted down the proposal that Saddleworth be incorporated within SELNEC (South East Lancashire and North East Cheshire), as the prototype for Greater Manchester was called. As he left the meeting he asked his old friend Joe Bradley why he had voted 'agin'. 'Well,' Joe replied, 'I wouldn't mind going in wi' Oldham, or even wi' Manchester, but I'm damned if I'm going in wi' a set of bloody initials!'

Saddleworth was eventually dragged protesting into Greater Manchester, but not without compromise. It acquired the only Parish Council within the new authority and retained its boundary signs, which feature prominently the white rose of Yorkshire. Perhaps most important of all to an area of cricket fanatics, the Yorkshire Cricket Club continues to recognise those born in Saddleworth as eligible for the county side, and every September a Yorkshire team still travels over the Pennines to play a combined Saddleworth XI in a one-day friendly match.

One Sunday in September 1979 a benefit match for England and Yorkshire player Chris Old was staged at Greenfield Cricket Club a mile or two from the Kenworthy's mill. John Kenworthy senior, comfortably dressed in his usual sports jacket, roll-neck sweater and fisherman's trilby, crossed the lane from Greenfield Bowling Club, known as 'the Gentlemen's', to watch the match in the low autumn sunshine, a slim panatella in his hand. Next to him his son John, the firm's designer, pointed out attractive bits of stroke-play to his eleven-year-old son Jonathan. The Kenworthy family rubbed shoulders easily with their own workpeople and with the scions of other woollen mill families like Jonathan Bradbury, the next generation of management at J. Bradbury & Sons, and Roger Tanner, already head of Tanner Brothers, a surviving cotton mill in Saddleworth. Roger Tanner, leading light in any number of Saddleworth's cultural activities, featured on this occasion as President of the Cricket Club and upheld his reputation as a natty dresser by wearing an old cricket blazer of his father's, the significance of its stripes apparently long since forgotten. It was an easy atmosphere that contrasted sharply with the great days of woollens when each mill owner ran his cricket team as competitively as his business. One of them, Robert Byrom, who died in 1880, was more interested in skills at cricket than weaving among potential employees. The story goes that he built for his team the row of twelve cottages that still stands next to the cricket field, and that from then on the workers' tenancy depended on their ability to stay in the side!

The casual visitor to many independent-minded communities often has to go further than just scratching the surface to see the differences for himself, but the divide between Saddleworth and Greater Manchester next door is immediately and visibly obvious from more than one angle. For instance, standing by the television transmitter on the hill above Greenfield station, to the south-west you see Oldham and Manchester beyond, a hazy plain interrupted by tower blocks and power stations. To the north and east, along the valley bottoms, lies a vivid green patchwork of irregular fields divided by dry-stone walls, meeting the grey-brown of the moorland tops in an irregular line of compromise. And each fold in the hills, each twist of the valley, holds another settlement of the original Saddleworth farming community. Along the valley bottom runs the main railway line from Huddersfield to Manchester. Down at that less romantic level as you emerge from the three-mile-long tunnel into Diggle, the unfolding of a series of dramatic views gives some idea of the shock these subsistence farming communities must have felt at the coming of canal, railway and Industrial Revolution. Diggle, which grew from a navvy settlement, clusters around the tunnel mouth, its gritstone weavers' cottages with their rows of second-floor windows to provide light for the looms matching those at the Yorkshire end of the tunnel. The valley itself is greener, but then come the mills dropped down in the green – Victorian edifices of Gothic proportions in this setting of low dry-stone walls. The mills have been there too long now to seem incongruous, but with the decline of the textile trade there is an air of melancholy about them, a reminder of the past rather than the

Telling reminders of how the industrial revolution came to Saddleworth

present. The disused grimy canal that meanders from its blocked tunnel through Diggle, Dobcross, Uppermill and Greenfield emphasises that feeling. Some mills are derelict, most converted to other uses; everyone knows the woollen textile trade is going the same way as King Cotton.

The mills first came to these steep Pennine valleys to make use of the fast-flowing tributaries that drained the almost inexhaustible supply of water from the damp moorlands above down into the long valley of the River Tame. The streams supplied these early fulling mills, themselves little bigger than cottages, both with power for their waterwheels and with a generous supply of soft water for scouring and cleansing the greasy woollen cloth. Whole strings of mills lined the banks of these small streams, each drawing off water in turn at small weirs according to their established rights. In many cases where mills still function these rights continue (on payment of a consideration to the Water Authority), and in dry summers remarks are still made only half-jokingly about keeping an eye open for slates surreptitiously placed over the higher outlets by those struggling to draw water lower down the stream!

Because of the mixed Danish and Saxon origins of the population, systems of inheritance varied, but the predominant system of split inheritance tended to make the farms progressively smaller and poorer, thereby strengthening the need for a second source of income like weaving. From among these families who had installed simple hand looms in their cottages, sprang the entrepreneurs who established their small fulling or finishing mills, bought in the raw lengths woven by their neighbours, finished them and sold them to the merchants in neighbouring towns. These early mill-owning families included both the Kenworthys, whose name appears on record in a will dated 1593, and the Bradburys, who claim to date back even further.

The earliest known residence and fulling mill of the Kenworthy family, known as 'Johnny Mill', was in the hills above Delph. But that disappeared under the waters of Castleshaw reservoir in the late-nineteenth century when the rapidly expanding cities made new demands on water supplies in the Pennines. Sitting in his functional but comfortably old-fashioned office, John Kenworthy senior ('Mr John' in his hearing, but out of earshot referred to affectionately throughout the mill as 'Father John'), looked over his glasses at great-uncle Frederick on the wall: 'He and my grandfather Charles came down here to Uppermill about 1878. This mill was proudly known then as "Buckley New Mill", and still is. To get started they probably rented a bit of the mill, installed a new steam engine, a few early carding machines and spinning mules, and fairly primitive scouring and drying machines. They've all been replaced now by slightly more modern stuff.' He laughed dryly. At the time we talked the mill was within days of closing down, which he knew but we did not: 'Those were the days when my grandfather used to go around smoking a cigar and paying the wages out of his trouser pocket. But it doesn't work quite that way now, does it?'

Even before the height of its activities Saddleworth must have been an impressive place to any businessman. A visitor in 1822 spoke of:

. . . about a hundred mills turned by the Tame and its tributary streams . . . Saddleworth is an interesting, though an uninviting part of the country, and the mountaineers of this region, like those of Switzerland, have a character peculiar to themselves. They are rude of speech but kind and hospitable in disposition, without many of the benefits of education, but of quick perception and sound judgement.

Gradually as steam replaced water power and made larger mills possible, all the successful firms moved to bigger premises along the valley bottom. The parish church of St Chad, standing on a site where there has been a church since 1215, illustrates the move. The last remains of the early mills litter the banks of the overgrown stream that flows past the church which, black and stark, now looks down on Uppermill through a fold in the hills. Once the focal point of the community, the church is now kept company only by a very popular free house, also called 'The Church', a rare example of a hearse house, and an ancient pair of stocks.

At the time the Kenworthys moved down to Uppermill their principal business seems to have been the weaving of shawls on Jacquard looms, though details are few since most of the firm's records were lost in a fire which gutted the mill in 1942. By the time John senior joined the firm in 1924 they were well into the manufacture of union shirtings which had seen them comfortably through the early part of the century and the First World War. The first signs of risky business came in the thirties when they began to make simple dress fabrics: 'Steadily we developed deeper and deeper into the fashion trade, and naturally ran into a lot more snags than when I was in the damn shirting trade. That had been killed by cheap imports from Japan, I think; the same sort of thing that's going to bump us all off today – imports from cheap labour countries. For a small firm you can't say we haven't tried to develop our export trade. We've done business with all the Scandinavian countries, Germany, France and Holland, with Australia, New Zealand, and a bit with America. We've tried to open up as many markets as we could handle with our sort of output. But in the fashion business the only thing that seems to have a charmed life is the tartans, and most of us in the trade have done a fair proportion of business in tartan fabrics.'

In spite of the broad hints of harder times to come from its owners, the casual observer of the mill itself could have been forgiven for putting down the gloomy prognosis to Yorkshire pessimism. In the weaving shed several dozen examples of the versatile Dobcross Loom, developed and patented locally at the end of the nineteenth century, clattered away under the watchful eyes of the women weavers, some of them minding four or five looms at a time. From the old wooden washing and scouring tubs festoons of tartan were constantly drawn upstairs to the drying room. In the finishing room the seventy-yard lengths of fancy tartans, tartan checks and plain weaves at every stage of completion were stacked high in all the available space. One clue to problems lay perhaps in the fact that few bales were alike – these days short runs and individual orders are seldom a paying proposition.

Both Kenworthys and Bradburys went into tartans in the late 1940s which, with the increasing popularity of its standard designs, became a useful 'bread-and-butter' line. In recent years tartans and tartan derivatives have been as much as sixty per cent of Kenworthy's output, with a good deal of it going to Scotland. Not long ago a Kenworthy weaver brought back from holiday in Scotland a length of 'particularly good tartan' only to have it pointed out that she had woven it herself! But even with standard designs there are many tartans, and the fashion trade soon demanded variations. This, coupled with the rising cost of raw materials, made even the building up of stocks in slack periods a risky proposition. So slack periods began to mean lay-offs and redundancies, and in a trade where skilled workers used to serve a seven-year apprenticeship, this dwindling pool of expertise could not be replenished in the good times. Young people no longer came in numbers into a trade where wages were depressed and an industry that was shrinking as obviously as wool in hot water. The simple economies of running Kenworthys demanded a through-put of more than two hundred pieces a week, and even with a Government order for one hundred thousand metres of khaki shirting and with some of their most loyal workers putting in phenomenal amounts of overtime, little impression was made on the level of thirty per cent under-production, or improvement on the loss of £2000 a week.

Four of the Kenworthy family were still working in the mill. The driving force was still undoubtedly John senior, paternal trouble-shooter among the workers and constantly about the mill in sports jacket and roll-neck sweater. He reckons to have operated most of the machines in his time, and even invented a Heath Robinson-like device involving bicycle-chain cogs, wire brushes and electric hair-trimmers to finish the selvages of tartans for hemless kilts.

After Cambridge and Huddersfield Technical College, his son John came into the firm on the 'creative side'. The technological

The weaving shed, Kenworthy's mill. *From left to right*: Fred, his son Mark,
John senior with his son John

course in textiles tended to confirm his discovery at an early age that
machinery fell to bits in his hands and that he would be better
employed in the family firm by making use of his artistic flair for
designing their textiles and then setting about selling them. This,
together with his feeling that he was not particularly cut out for
dealing with people, tended to put more distance between him and
most of the workers, though he has been no less involved in all aspects
of the company's fortunes than his father.

The organisational side of the firm fell to Fred Kenworthy, Works
Director and John senior's nephew, indistinguishable in dress and
speech from his employees. His son Mark, shy and quiet, had only
recently started with a fair degree of optimism on the 'shop floor' as a
storeman, taking in good part the friendly jibes from his workmates
that the girls only chased him because 'one day all this will be yours'.

If John senior illustrates the lack of distance in this community
between employer and employee, his son John's friendship with
Jonathan Bradbury, ten years his junior and working his way up the

sales department of the rival firm, shows that after office hours, competition in business can still take second place to community kinship. In the bar of 'The Church', where both of them put away a pint or two on a fairly regular basis, John Kenworthy pointed out that secrecy between the mills was not what it used to be: 'In the old days I suppose we should probably not have got together as much as we do, but on the whole now we know a lot more than we let on about each other's business. I even do quite a bit of designing using Bradbury's colour yarns. It makes it easy if we run out of yarn – I just nip down the road and buy a bit of theirs.'

At one time Jonathan's wife Judith worked as John's secretary, but although one mutual customer was so absolutely convinced Judith was taking Kenworthy's secrets back to Bradburys that she became known in both firms as Mata Hari, as Jonathan pointed out, her loyalty was such that he learned more from John than from his wife! Jonathan went on: 'It's very rarely that you get people moving from one factory to another. I can think of two spinners who work for John who are always egging me on by asking if there are any jobs going down at our place and I say, yes, come on down, but they never do and they never will.'

In the light of what was to happen only a few days later, the tone of the conversation became altogether more serious when we asked about the possibility of a merger as a way out of present difficulties. They glanced at each other, then John Kenworthy plunged in: 'It's not something we've never thought about, but really we're too closely aligned in what we produce for that sort of thing to happen. It would be OK if we were making tartans and they were making plain piece styles, for example. Then you'd have two totally different things that would go together quite well.'

Jonathan spelt it out: 'If it worked, one way or another, one bit would have to be absorbed, wouldn't it? We'd have to shut one section down.'

If mill owners and managers find it necessary to hedge their conversation about with ifs and buts simply to maintain for as long as possible the credibility of their firms, the mill workers are less in-hibited about giving practical expression to their doubts about the future. The head loom tuner at Kenworthys, Brian Taylor, a dark, plain-speaking Yorkshireman, has begun reversing the process by which his forebears became textile workers, and turned again to the land. Obviously to escape to the green fields and dry-stone walls of his small-holding in Diggle has been an attractive proposition after the clatter and grime of the mill, but at the time we met him, the few beef cattle and sheep he was rearing and the sheepdogs he was training were beginning to look much more like an insurance policy than a hobby. Brian lives with his wife Ann and their three growing children in a traditional three-storey weaver's cottage, blackened stone outside and cosily modernised inside. House prices have soared in this attract-ive corner of the hills, so the Taylors need to make a bob or two to pay off the mortgage, let alone supplement the consistently low wages even for skilled workers in the textile trade, and provide for an uncertain future.

Fortunately the throw-back to earlier generations is strong enough for both of them to relish a way of life that means hard work and the open air. Brian expresses it in his enthusiasm for training sheepdogs: 'I enjoy bringing up a little pup and watching it make its first moves, taking notice of the sheep and watching them run round. From then on it's very rewarding, because for every day you can see something being achieved.'

Ann too lives a full life apart from running a happy household for the children: 'We're not really the sitting-down sort of people. We're only happy when we're doing something, and we enjoy everything we do. We keep saying we'll perhaps cut down, but we always end up finding different things to do.'

In Ann's case that used to mean a good deal of mending for Kenworthys or Bradburys of unfinished fabric straight from their looms. The Taylors had re-equipped their top-floor room, which would once have housed the cottage weaver's looms, so that Ann could run the seventy-yard lengths over rollers fixed to the ceiling as she repaired the broken threads and faults in each piece. It was an expertise she had acquired as a girl after her mother had talked her into taking up mending, when, like Brian, she discovered that jobs outside textiles were hard to come by. Now, with the decline in textiles Ann has begun to turn her attention to other practical and profitable ways of occupying her time. Over the past few years she has completed certificated courses in sheep husbandry, tractor-driving and dry-stone walling. Recently the mending room has begun to look more like a bakery as Ann makes dozens of pies for her weekly stall on Uppermill market. Every Wednesday Brian helps to set up the stall he built for her and by eleven o'clock all the fruit and savoury pies she has time to make have been sold. Whether this little enterprise can continue to expand remains to be seen, but as Ann says: 'The mending would still be a good standby if I were to poison all Uppermill with my pies, but let's face it, nobody's going to make anything in this world working for other people are they?'

Like his father before him, Brian began his working life as an apprentice fitter at Dobcross Looms down the valley: 'My mother wanted me to go in for sheet metal working, but there was nothing suitable at the time. So the Dobcross Loom works was the last hope, type of thing, for me. But once there, I reckon I've had a good life out of the textiles.'

His father Jack Taylor, who lives just a few doors away and shares his son's passion for sheep and dogs, was an 'out-fitter' erecting Dobcross looms all over the world. He was literally born into the trade himself in Russia in 1915. His father had gone there to erect fifty Dobcross looms and had stayed on when he was offered a job as weaving manager: 'I was born in what was Petrograd in those days, what's Leningrad today, but we had to leave when the Revolution came along. My mother came home first with the children, and my father stayed until he had to get out. He had to leave all the furniture; he lost almost everything he had there. So he had to start afresh here with Dobcross Looms.'

Before the firm closed down in the sixties and Jack moved to Kenworthys as a loom tuner, he had travelled the world as an out-fitter, erecting looms that were an unrivalled example of British technology. As so often though, there was some sitting on laurels, and it was left to continental manufacturers to copy and improve our looms. Now that the British market is being flooded with cheap textiles coming in the other direction, Jack was inclined to agree that he may have had a hand in digging the grave of our textile industry: 'I suppose that's what it amounts to. We definitely exported a lot of our expertise, and we're still doing it. All these universities, Leeds, Bradford, are full of foreign students learning the trade and taking it back home with them. I think the future looks a bit bleak. Over in Yorkshire it's proved to be a dying industry. The cotton in Lancashire went first, and when the cotton mills were closing down, we never really thought the woollen would go the same way, but it definitely has.'

Brian is equally candid about what he sees as the bleak future prospects of the industry: 'We've been saying for ten to fifteen years that the industry was living hand-to-mouth, but years ago the seasonal slackness in the fashion trade was from September till after Christmas. Now there can be a slump at any time at all. Then again, there are no young people coming into the industry for the simple reason that they can see it's more or less a dead end job. I wouldn't like to think that any of my children would be going into it. From my point of view, at thirty-nine, I'd like to think that the textiles would last me another twenty years, but I honestly don't think they will. So I say to myself, the firm might be better going bust now, making me redundant so that I'm at a better age for retraining. If I had a wishing bone, I'd like to wish that if anything happened to Kenworthy's, I could get somewhere with a few more acres of land to farm, but you see in this particular area now, every bit of land is bought up by people with horses.'

The Saddleworth environment is close enough to urban life for monied refugees from the cities to be tolerated, and welcoming enough for many of the new arrivals quite quickly to take an active part in community affairs, but Saddleworth has been a self-contained society for too long to be unaware of the tears being made in its fabric. Roger Tanner still points out that although there is no cinema, dance hall or bingo in Saddleworth, it has about twenty-four youth groups, seventy registered charities (including cultural and social groups of every description) and almost as many pubs, so that even now few people leave the area to seek their evening's entertainment. Yet at the same time the inference of more fundamental changes is contained in Brian Taylor's references to 'people with horses', in the disappearance of tap-rooms in the locals, and, since assimilation into the Metropolitan District of Oldham, in the appearance on Saddleworth's hillsides of conspicuous estates of little boxes.

Now that children no longer have to follow their parents into the mills, it is the younger generation who live here for the atmosphere rather than the work who are most concerned about change. Peter Ashworth, at thirty-three, was content to look after yarn supply to the looms at Kenworthy's, not because he particularly liked the job but because it enabled him to live and work in Saddleworth, where his interests lie and he feels he belongs. He was actually born beyond the boundary, but his wife Janet came from an old Saddleworth family, the Charlesworths, and on her mother's side is related to the Mallalieus, a Huguenot family who came to Saddleworth in the 1600s and still run one of the woollen mills along the valley in Delph.

Some years ago, Peter was lucky enough to acquire an old terraced cottage on the hill above Uppermill before every last derelict barn was being bought up by outsiders, but now he sees young couples looking for rented property being forced to accept council flats in Oldham, while the better-off older generation of Lancastrians seem to be positively encouraged to move in the opposite direction. What Peter, and many young locals, fear is the prospect of a Saddleworth that is little more than a smart residential suburb of Oldham, a character change which he says would eventually force him reluctantly to leave the area.

For the moment though the Ashworths remain, quietly but stubbornly determined to keep the local spirit alive among their generation. Saddleworth has long been culturally aware of its own identity, seen in its four-yearly Arts Festival, its thriving Historical Society, renowned brass band contests and its own museum and art gallery, but the Ashworths' interest is in the folk tradition, altogether more at grass roots level. Peter played a major part in revitalising the Saddleworth Morris Men and is now their Squire. Janet continually researches new dances with local connections, and a few years ago during research for a polytechnic thesis came across references to the Rushcart Ceremony, last seen in Saddleworth about 1919. Since 1975 Peter and the Saddleworth Morris Men have revived the event each August Bank Holiday.

Rushbearing in Saddleworth goes back to pagan days, but in Christian times involved the ceremonial pulling of cart-loads of rushes each autumn from all of the hamlets up to the Heights Church at Delph and Saddleworth Church at Uppermill, where the rushes would be spread deep on the earthen floors for winter warmth. After the flagging of the church floors in the early-nineteenth century the custom continued as part of the Uppermill Wakes, and the rushes were sold off for animal bedding, but as the ceremony lost its religious connections, the Uppermill Wakes or 'Longwood Thump' became what Peter describes as 'a boozy do and a fighting do' with good chapel folk like Janet's family keeping their children indoors.

The rush carts finally died out with the departure of the young men during the First World War, but in 1975 Peter Ashworth cajoled the

Preparing the rushcart in the yard of the Commercial Inn. Peter Ashworth is directing operations from on high

morris men into building just one cart, though it did not win universal acclaim, as he remembers: 'One old bloke walked round the corner, took one look at it and said. "Nowt like one, lad!" and I just thought, "Oh bloody hell, after all that."'

The 1979 example looked impressive enough to justify all the work, bearing a strong resemblance to the photographs of vintage carts in the 1880s. For weeks beforehand the morris men, their wives and girlfriends, had hacked their way with sickles across every boggy patch high on the moors above Saddleworth. Each evening whatever

The finished rushcart on its Saturday tour of Saddleworth pubs

the weather, they collected more bundles to make up the one-and-a-half tons they needed for the cart in the yard of the Commercial Inn, getting back in time for a quick bout of clog-dancing and a slow pint or two before closing-time.

At August Bank Holiday weekend, morris teams from as far afield as Preston and Coventry poured into Saddleworth for what is rapidly becoming a major event in the clog dancer's calendar. On the Saturday, up to a hundred sturdy young men, with another thirty or so behind as the brakes, pulled the cart-load of rushes round the district, one of their number on top lowering a copper kettle at every hostelry for fresh supplies! On the Sunday morning they took the cart at a licking pace up the hill past enthusiastic crowds to a packed St Chad's where the young vicar, Rev. John Sykes, received a few token bundles of rushes at the altar. Afterwards the sloping square outside the church and 'The Church' was packed with spectators for the dancing and the wrestling, gurning and clog-stepping competitions. It was very noticeable how many people knew each other. Apart from the visiting morris teams and their friends, this was a very local crowd.

During the summer Peter and Janet Ashworth had taken the financial plunge of tackling the long overdue renovation of their cottage. By September Janet was expecting a baby and though the work was well advanced, it was obviously going to be a race to straighten out the house and pay the bills before the baby arrived in February and Janet's income from her work in a local craft industry ceased. The sudden closure of Kenworthys' mill was to come as a real blow to the Ashworths, raising the possibility of an earlier move from the area by necessity rather than choice.

By the end of September the signs at the mill were ominous. Meetings were taking place behind locked doors, and one morning all the directors, wearing suits, went off to see the bank manager in Oldham. In conversation the Kenworthys were obviously in pessimistic mood; it was a time for reflection on the past. In the room his wife calls the 'play pen' John senior played his Steinway grand for us, a glass of whisky on the side, and thought about what else he might have been: 'Not a musician, because I'm not good enough – you need an absolute flair to be any use. Not a schoolmaster, I'd have gone mad. One particular friend, one of Rutherford's bright boys, got very annoyed with me because he thought I ought to have been a physicist. But I knew I wasn't quite bright enough for that. I'm not sure I'm bright enough to run a woollen mill either.' He laughed, then his head came up defiantly and he wagged his finger: 'Not under the present conditions, not under the present conditions!' Then, with some regret: 'But I don't think nature intended me for the job really, any more than it did John. Somehow I think he'd have been happier in a better context.'

John junior soon made it clear that, if anything, it was the family tradition, not his father, that had pushed him into the business, rather than a career in journalism, or advertising, or acting, all of which seem to have more than crossed his mind: 'It always seemed almost inevitable that I would gravitate into the mill. I suppose if I'd had any raging ambition to be something else, I could have gone ahead and done it. In fact I'm quite sure my father quite often said, "You'd be a bloody fool if you come into this business!" I suppose my father has always been the dominant personality in the mill, but that doesn't mean he stopped us from having ideas and following them through. There have been occasions when I wished to hell he'd not been there, but by and large he's an agreeable patriarch.'

We asked whether being a mill-owner still seemed to confer any special status in the community: 'I think there's still a bit of mystique about it, but there shouldn't be because, well, we feel we're really rather less well-off than the average shop-keeper these days. As they say locally, "I don't think there's owt down for owning a mill!"'

His son Jonathan might presumably be expected to tread the same path as his father: 'He'll be very cross if he doesn't get to Cambridge certainly, but after that he wants to be a marine biologist at the moment, and I won't stand in his way. Really I wouldn't want him to come into the mill. It's a very difficult industry and I just don't think the rewards are right any more for the effort that goes into it.'

It was just twelve days after that conversation that the Kenworthys told their workers the mill would have close. Most of the debts were cleared by the sale of the mill and its contents, though in the case of the venerable Dobcross looms the sledgehammers soon followed the auctioneer's hammer as they were knocked down at £20 each for scrap. Even the no-nonsense representative of the plastic foam company, preparing to take over the mill, confessed to feeling distressed by such destruction.

In spite of old loyalties these were circumstances in which quite a few of Kenworthys' workers did look for work along the street at Bradburys. But even for the successful ones, their reprieve was to be short-lived. Nine months after Kenworthys, Bradburys announced that they too were to close. So two local mills, traditional employers of Saddleworth people for more than a century, had succumbed in less than a year to pressures that were closing Northern textile mills at the rate of one a week.

Hoghton

'The Tower is like a good woman. You know you love her and yet you're driven mad by her.'

The sombre crenellated walls of Hoghton Tower have dominated the road between Preston and Blackburn since 1565. Set on a steep, wooded hill in the rolling landscape of rural Lancashire, the Tower, a fortified manor house, is still the central point of an estate that once stretched as far as the Fylde coast. The de Hoghton family were in Lancashire long before the present house was built. In fact, the 'roots' of the de Hoghtons are thought to be far older than the first written record – the name Hoctonam on a deed of 1160.

Today, Sir Bernard de Hoghton holds the title to one of the oldest baronetcies in England. Since Sir Bernard took over the administration of the estate, one famous event in the history of Hoghton Tower has been commemorated by a banquet. King James VI of Scotland and I of England visited Hoghton in 1617, there in the great hall he 'knighted' a loin of beef, and the term 'sirloin' passed into common English usage. Now up to three hundred paying guests attend to celebrate the occasion. As the loin of beef is brought in, Sir Bernard rises to speak, not to invite the company to set to and devour the beef, but to remind them that in accordance with modern custom the loin is to be raffled later in the evening. The proceeds will be added to the night's takings, a small contribution towards keeping the old building afloat above a rising tide of dry rot and taxation.

The de Hoghton family are no strangers to the financial problems attendant on the aristocracy. It is a nice irony that as a result of the original three days of feasting Sir Bernard's ancestor, Sir Richard Hoghton, alias 'Bluff Dick', spent a year in the Fleet Prison while the debts he had incurred were paid off. Sir Richard was perhaps one of the luckier ones, for King James had such a reputation for descending with an enormous retinue on the hospitality of his unfortunate nobles that some are said to have burnt their ancestral homes to the ground in advance rather than fall victim to the consequences of a royal visit!

Gatehouse of Hoghton Tower

The cost of maintaining a large estate in modern times has made things difficult for many titled families, but for the de Hoghtons there were additional problems of estate duties when Sir Bernard's older half-brother, Sir Anthony, died unexpectedly in February 1978. Sir Bernard, as he now became on succeeding to the baronetcy, has avoided a similar fate to that suffered by the family's first baronet – he draws a salary from the stockbroking firm he works for in London.

Sir Bernard spends weekends in Lancashire, but the majority of weekdays find him, brolly and briefcase in hand, back among the commuters to the City. His working day is spent in the Stock Exchange tower block, in the offices of de Zoete and Bevan, one of the City's oldest and biggest stockbrokers. The firm has more than thirty partners, though as yet, being a relatively new arrival, Sir Bernard is not one of them. Closed-circuit television keeps him in touch with information such as prices on the Stock Exchange floor or currency exchange rates around the world. Much of his time is spent on the telephone to the European money markets of Frankfurt, Paris and

Milan. The ease with which Sir Bernard may move millions in paper money contrasts strangely with the thousands in hard cash he urgently needs to raise at home.

Since his succession as the fourteenth baronet the almost weekly commuting between Lancashire and the capital, by car or cheap weekend rail returns, has undoubtedly increased the personal pressures, but Sir Bernard says he finds his dual life stimulating: 'I enjoy living in London and working in the City. The City work means mental anxiety and not much physical hard work, which is what the weekends offer me. I'm only too happy to get filthy in the woods cutting trees down or transporting logs, because I'm not having to think is this going up or is that going down. There's no worry to it, just beautiful hard work; you come back at night, drop into bed and that's it.' One wonders whether his grandfather, who hunted in these woods with George V, would have approved.

Records in Lancashire for a hundred years after the Norman conquest are extremely limited, but the first Hoghton home on or around the present site is thought to have been a peel tower. It was built by the de Hoghtons' early Norman ancestors, the de Walters, who arrived in England with William the Conqueror. The family's Saxon forebears, described by Sir Bernard as 'much kinder and rather more interesting', and said by at least one pedigree to have been related to Earl Leofric and Lady Godiva, probably lived close by the River Darwen in the valley below, but the Normans, being conquerors, felt it more appropriate, and perhaps safer, to build their house, or at least a refuge, on the hill. By about 1300 the family was well established locally, and it is from this period that the Hoghtons began serving with some regularity as Sheriffs of Lancashire. The shields of all the Sheriffs down to the present time are displayed in Lancaster Castle, and the distinctive horizontal black and silver bars of the Hoghton coat-of-arms stand out at regular intervals among the rest.

The de Hoghtons had long served the King as Knights 'banneret', whose duties included holding the royal standard in battle, when James I created Richard Hoghton the first baronet in 1611. Naturally enough when King James arrived six years later on an official visit with his huge entourage, Sir Richard had little option but to 'roll out the red carpet', which he apparently did literally – from top to bottom of the hill. In three days of hunting and feasting the royal visitors drank him out of the Rhenish wine for which his cellars were famous. The King left the de Hoghtons in debt but with their most famous story. Sir Bernard tells it with relish: 'The King had really enjoyed his hunting and the food was so good that having enjoyed the roast beef at the feast, he asked for the loin to be brought over to him. The King stood up, placed his sword on the beef and said: "Arise, Sir Loin!" Everyone cheered – you can imagine, they were half-tight anyway – and of course it stuck because everyone at the time thought it was such a good joke.' The court painter, who was present, dutifully did a quick sketch, a copy of which hangs in the Great Hall. The original is now in the USA.

For the ancestral home of such an old-established family, Hoghton Tower is noticeably lacking in major paintings and family portraits. The de Hoghtons have suffered many strokes of bad luck over the centuries, but one of the cruellest was the destruction in 1870 of most of the family pictures and much of the family plate. These had been stored for 'safe-keeping' in the Pantechnicon in London, and were destroyed by fire. 'So, because of that,' says Sir Bernard simply, 'we don't really know what our earlier ancestors looked like.' Nevertheless, in three of the portraits that survive, family features are clearly discernible – straight nose, high cheekbones, determined chin – but the de Hoghtons pictured could hardly have been more disparate in character. Thomas Hoghton, who pre-dated the baronetcy and took three years to build the present house, eventually left the country and died in Liège rather than give up his Catholicism on Queen Elizabeth's demand; Sir Charles de Hoghton, the fourth baronet and a nonconformist, was at Cambridge with Isaac Newton and later built Preston Grammar School; while by contrast Sir Henry Philip, the seventh baronet, helped the Dashwoods found the Hellfire Club and hardly enhanced the family's reputation by losing Bootle, part of their lands near Liverpool, at the gaming tables.

In the twentieth century Henry Philip's grandson Sir James, the eleventh baronet and Sir Bernard's grandfather, showed a more creative turn of mind by inventing the trolley bus, installing electricity in the house and a hydraulic ram at the foot of the hill to provide a pumped water supply. However, two generations later Sir Anthony was showing a marked inclination to return to the leisured existence of Henry Philip, and it was his neglect of the property that left the Tower with its present problems to fall heavily into the lap of his half-brother Bernard. Since Bernard was the third son of Sir Cuthbert, his succession to the baronetcy was unexpected. Anthony became the thirteenth baronet in 1958, but lived to enjoy the title only until 1978, while the second son, Charles, died in 1971.

In 1958 Sir Anthony inherited a house that had been progressively improved and restored over the immediately preceding generations. Certainly in the past the de Hoghtons had neglected the Tower to the point of leaving it deserted for years on end (at one time in the early nineteenth century it was occupied for a time by squatting Lancashire weavers), but by the 1950s it was in good condition after Sir Cuthbert had put to rights the ravages of the Second World War years. As with so many country houses, other users had priority then, and wartime occupants included a flight of RAF pilots and a group of nuns.

Sir Cuthbert had anticipated Anthony's obvious lack of interest in Hoghton Tower by placing all the family records in the County Record Office in Preston (where they can still be seen), but after Sir Cuthbert's death lack of interest took on a more destructive nature. Sir Anthony began to live increasingly abroad, and as farm rental income did not match his rather extravagant tastes, certain family assets had to be sold. One such episode concerned the famous table. One day a large van arrived and workmen armed with saws announced they had come to remove from the banqueting hall the long table on which James I had knighted the loin. Since the table had been constructed in the hall itself from the trunk of a single tree, the only way in which it could be removed was in pieces. Fortunately this act of vandalism was prevented by the physical intervention of the present baronet and his mother. Over the next few years Sir Anthony's finances and his management of them steadily improved, but he was eventually persuaded to sever his connections with the house. Bernard took over the care of the Tower, and immediately began to tackle the problems of restoration work. The first step was to have an architects' inspection. They discovered massive infestation by dry rot, of which there were four major outbreaks. Between 1956 and 1974 the house had been allowed to fall into a state of neglect which is still being dealt with.

Two factors have enabled Sir Bernard to begin the restoration work in earnest. Firstly, there is an arrangement with the Historic Buildings Council whereby they give a fifty per cent grant on all work, providing the family raises the other fifty per cent. Secondly, because

Great Hall, Hoghton. The table at which King James I 'knighted' the loin of beef is on the right

of the educational value of tours by schools and other organisations, a charitable trust has been set up for eighty years to which the house has been leased.

Sir Bernard, his shirt-sleeves rolled up, took us on a swift tour of the main trouble spots. His affection for the house was at its most apparent when he clambered up into the roofs with a torch to show us the sheer size of their timbers, or up on to the high point of the gatehouse to show their construction from the outside: 'Looked at from here the house is typically Tudor with a lot of the roofs pointing in towards each other. They're all higgledy-piggledy, in fact an aerial view would show that no two wings abut at ninety degrees. Underneath the stone slab tiling the roofs are supported by massive timbers that are actually whole trees, and access is very difficult. It's rather like being in a mine with only small holes in the stone dividing walls that take some of the weight, and there's very little natural light. So dry rot

Lower courtyard, Hoghton Tower

can easily spread without necessarily being seen, and then suddenly it's all around you.' Sir Bernard is quite clear about the size of his responsibility: 'I think the major problem we have is not just the maintenance of the house but more so our ability as a family to manage taxation. The family is not actually getting paid for the restoration work at all. Not that that bothers us, because we think of it as saving something both for the family and for the nation. But when death duties strike you, you know all about it. They can destroy in one year something it has taken a family countless generations to achieve.'

Sir Bernard's coming to terms with the practical problems of his duties have necessarily been rapid since February 1978. Following the death of his half-brother, he was catapulted into a completely new situation. Fortunately Sir Bernard prefers to be busy, so his many activities at weekends when the house is open to visitors are relentless and varied. After the trip from London, Saturday may well be spent cutting logs for sale to swell the Restoration Fund, erecting fences or visiting tenant farmers with his agent. Most of Sunday, at least in the summer, is involved with visitors, but although he is not averse to taking parties round himself, Sir Bernard rather prefers to leave the guided tours to his mother – 'She does it so much better.' On these open days they rely very heavily on an army of local volunteers whose continuing interest and loyalty is obviously vital to the family's restoration plans: 'It's sometimes very tricky on a Bank Holiday when some of our volunteers naturally enough have divided loyalties over whether to take the family to the seaside or come up here, and instead of twenty only fifteen appear. In the last few hours before opening time there's a most almighty shindy of telephone calls to make up the numbers. Mind you, I'm very lucky in that my mother is a wonderful organiser. She is largely responsible for what you might call the general administration of the house.'

Major Richard Adams, Sir Bernard's stepfather, is also part of the team, taking the money at the gate and jovially threatening noisy children with the dungeons. He also supervises a team of volunteer marshals who pack visitors into the car park, more properly referred to as the 'Tilting Green'. Inside the inner courtyard is a tearoom with bright crockery and fresh posies on every table, staffed by a group of local ladies. Mrs Adams, Sir Bernard's mother, gives them a hand between taking parties round the house.

As the visitors troop round with her there is evident pride in her retelling of the impressive and colourful history into which she has married. From the 'Guinea Room' where Henry Philip lost Bootle to the Derby family, she leads them to the family ballroom, where a changing selection of Hoghton documents from the Preston Record office is displayed. The Hoghton documents are wonderfully varied, dating back to the time of William the Conqueror and King Stephen. But in her tours, Mrs Adams wisely concentrates on those items and events that everyone is supposed to remember: 'Starting here, Henry IV is granting a licence to found a chantry in 1406, and here's Queen Elizabeth I's signature in 1598. Here, Charles I is granting a general pardon to Sir Gilbert de Hoghton. He was being "had up" for treason and insurrection and all sorts of things, but Charles I forgave him. Ironically it was Charles who had his head chopped off.'

In spite of her enthusiasm, Mrs Adams finds she has inherited a seven-days-a-week job which she describes as 'living over the shop': 'My late husband was a historian and he just adored this place, and naturally he passed on the love of it to me. I felt when he died that it was my responsibility to carry on. I was nineteen when I came here from the village of Walton-le-Dale, I had fallen in love with a Hoghton, and from then on the history of the family unfolded every day. I think one accepts things much more readily at that age, so for example I didn't even think it was a very big house. People used to say to me, "Aren't you amazed at the size of that house!" But there was just so much to do and so many things I wanted to change after the nuns and the Air Force left.'

Mrs Adams, like her son, is under no illusion about the less romantic side of the restoration effort: 'Having the house open to the public produces a lot of money, but with the restoration going on at the same time, as soon as the money comes in, it goes out. And besides the vast amount of money we have to find for dry rot, there's now the question of death duties which have to be paid. In the past perhaps the house was a millstone round the estate's neck, but it isn't now. The house is completely self-supporting, and has to be.'

As she remembers how the work began, Mrs Adams' fighting talk reveals resilience tempered by a sense of humour. 'When we started the restoration a band of volunteers came in to help us, and we all joined in. We put up scaffolding and washed the panelling and polished it, and did all the painting ourselves too. And afterwards I remember we had fish and chips. King James I would have been quite horrified at the goings on in the state parts of the house.'

Just as the family's personal and political fortunes have fluctuated down the years, there are echoes too of a turbulent religious past. In the seventeenth and early-eighteenth centuries, the years of Catholic repression, this part of Lancashire was a hotbed of religious dissent. Priests crept furtively down hidden lanes to celebrate the forbidden Mass, and after the Jacobite rebellion secret 'Mass houses' sprang up, visited by priests who would never say where the next Mass was to be celebrated. Often, clean washing hung out on the hedges would be the only clue to the faithful.

The Church of St Joseph, Brindle, built inconspicuously in 1786, looks, from the outside at least, more Quaker than Catholic. Even after the days of persecution it still paid Catholics not to draw attention to themselves. Today the church is full, the car park packed, and as often as he can Sir Bernard attends Mass and reads the lesson.

But the de Hoghtons have not always remained Catholic, for along with many other Catholic families they parted from Rome in Tudor times. Around 1569, soon after he had completed the Tower, Thomas Hoghton went into exile in Flanders rather than give up the faith, taking his son Thomas with him. Thomas the younger studied at

Douai College, was ordained a priest and returned to the dangerous task of ministering to the faithful in Lancashire. He was soon arrested and flung into Salford jail, where it can be assumed he died, since his name disappears from the prison lists in January 1584. Meanwhile Queen Elizabeth I had raised Thomas the elder's nephew Richard at court as a Protestant, and he succeeded to the title in 1589 after his father, Thomas' younger brother had been killed in an affray with a neighbouring landowner. Sir Richard (Bluff Dick) Hoghton soon became known as a scourge of the Catholics and, being a favourite of James I, was created the first baronet in 1611.

The eighteenth-century de Hoghtons were strongly non-conformist, either building or founding a number of chapels in the area. The Wesleyan chapel in Hoghton village dates from the end of the century, but between 1717 and 1729 Hoghton Tower itself had been listed as a Presbyterian chapel. In contrast the early nineteenth-century baronets devoted themselves to the pastimes of gambling and cockfighting in preference to religion (another period when the Tower and estates fell into neglect) but, by reaction perhaps, Sir Bernard's late Victorian ancestors turned High Anglican and built what was surprisingly Hoghton's first parish church. It was Sir Bernard's father Sir Cuthbert who finally led the family back to Roman Catholicism:

'My father became a Catholic about 1900 when he was reading History at Magdalene College, Oxford. It was there he met an extremely interesting Italian Jesuit and became a Catholic at a time when it was not a very fashionable thing to be.' Whether by impulse, conscience or sheer perversity it seems that few de Hoghtons could ever have been accused of being plain conformists!

The combination of varied religious adherence, lack of a parish church and discontinuous occupation of the Tower itself has left the family with an unusual problem. As Sir Bernard points out: 'The de Hoghtons are buried all over the place. Several are in Preston parish church where the chancel is divided with another family. Some are buried at St Leonard's, Walton-le-Dale, and others are in the church-yard of St James the Less in Samlesbury. It's rather sad that we have no special vault or chantry.'

Most of the family's lands in these outlying areas have long since been sold off, but the Hoghton estate is still some two thousand two hundred acres, split up into twenty-odd holdings, which are overseen by Sir Bernard's agent, John Forrester. Over recent years about three hundred acres have been sold off and now more will probably have to go to pay death duties. Sir Bernard, though, is anxious to retain what he can, so in an attempt to get to grips with another aspect of his inheritance he administers estate affairs at weekends in company with John Forrester.

After high finance in the City, building maintenance and tourism, Sir Bernard is now involved in estate management, which was his mother's area of study at the time she first met Sir Cuthbert. Besides revealing a good working knowledge of farming trends and discussing the potential of the various units, Sir Bernard shows his personal interest in the tenants and their families, whose older members have, after all, known him since he ran round the village as a small boy. The talk in the car is of the Stringmans whose Home Farm is to have additional buildings and extra land incorporated from another farmhouse which is to be sold off, of the Hargreaves of Windmill Farm, and of the 'sound' unit that is the Cross's farm. When Sir Bernard and John Forrester call in on George Clayton and his family at Green Farm, the business of the visit, the reslating of the old stone barn, soon melts into an informal chat about the high price of beef cattle, and George's son Raymond who is showing more interest in clocks and watches than farming. Raymond has recently restored an old tower clock up at the house and now he is complimented on one he has just installed in the gable end of the old barn.

The next stop is New Wicken House Farm, home of 'senior' tenant Tom Livesey and his family. There is nothing remarkable about the Liveseys' hundred-acre farm with its dairy herd and couple of thousand battery hens, but Tom himself is a living reminder that it is not only aristocrats who have distinguished pedigrees. Records show that the Liveseys probably arrived in these parts about the same time as the de Hoghtons. There is a reference to a Tom Livesey in Hoghton papers of 1656, and traditionally the eldest son of the family has always been called Tom. Nowadays, 'young Tom', a strapping lad in his twenties and a keen Rugby Union player, is in partnership with his father.

1978 will be a year to remember for the Liveseys, as the date when the family managed to put the clock back several hundred years. In the mid-seventeenth century they had been yeoman farmers, owning their own land, and in 1978, just before Sir Bernard's succession,

Tom and his son were given the opportunity to buy back their land from the estate and cease to be tenants. On the face of it Tom is very matter-of-fact about his new position but there is a twinkle in his eye that shows he must have jumped at the chance. 'I really have the feeling I've followed my ancestors on, and I think it's grand. There's nothing in a name really though, is there, but I'm glad we bought it. It feels better; I'm a landowner now, aren't I, one of the rich.' He laughs at himself, and then goes on seriously. 'I still like to feel I have a contact with the Tower though. Mustn't lose that.'

Over the years the relationship between the Hoghtons and Liveseys seems to have been anything but the feudal one of master and man: 'My grandad used to have some rare times with old Sir James, Sir Bernard's grandfather. Grandad used to go up to the Tower for drinks and the story had it they used to wrestle together. In my father's day when you paid your rent you got a meal, twice a year in May and November. And quite often they'd have a few drinks with the tenants and even go off on the spree with them. They always seemed to like the farmers. They didn't do a lot to the property but they didn't charge big rents, and they'd allow you to do anything you wanted. We put up a couple of buildings and they'd no objections.'

In the summer of 1978 Tom and the remaining tenants of the estate were invited with their wives to an informal party at the Tower to mark Sir Bernard's accession to the title, and Tom was called upon to propose a toast. His remarks were typically concise: 'Sir Bernard, Lady de Hoghton, ladies and gentlemen, I'm very honoured today to propose a toast to Sir Bernard on becoming the fourteenth baronet of Hoghton. I am sure that he will keep in close contact with the people of Hoghton, especially the tenants. And I hope that he can keep the Tower. We all wish him luck.' And there can be no doubt they all meant it, but Tom, the shrewd Lancashire farmer, could not resist a wry comment afterwards: 'It needs a lot of money spending on it to keep it in good shape, but I wouldn't mind buying it if it ever came empty. Make a lovely hotel, wouldn't it!' Hoghtons past and present can almost be heard trembling at the thought!

Both Sir Bernard and his mother are adamant that the Tower must never become a financial burden on the estate, so the books for each are kept separately, with Mrs Adams concentrating her efforts on the house. And she emphasises that she has more than just enthusiasm to offer: 'I was a tomboy at heart and I liked nothing better than climbing trees and digging ditches. So when I started work in the estate office, I began with measuring land, drainage, that sort of thing, and studied estate management on my own and at night school. And I really looked forward to the half-yearly rent days, when the farmers came to pay their rents . . .'

At that time of course she had no idea how valuable her intimate knowledge of house and estate were to become, or how heavy the responsibilities that would land in her lap: 'Sometimes I'm very optimistic. I think we're breaking the back of the work and that we're going to be here for another thousand years perhaps. But then something goes wrong, hopelessly wrong, like the fact that death duties now have to be found, and you just have to start all over again. That's the way it goes, I'm afraid. I can't see an end to it, but I'm really grateful that Bernard is as much in love with the place as I am. I'd love to see all the work finished before I die.'

On Sunday 11 June, members of the Sealed Knot gathered at Hoghton to recreate a scene from the family's chequered history. The Sealed Knot specialise in recreating battles from the English Civil War, and Hoghton in the 1640s was the setting for two major events. In 1642 Sir Gilbert Hoghton, the second baronet, defeated a large body of Parliamentarians at the little-known battle of West Hoghton, some miles away. In the following year Roundhead forces captured the Tower, but, having given safe passage to Sir Gilbert and his men, their leader and sixty of his troopers were killed when a booby-trapped powder magazine exploded and brought down the central tower on top of them. The only reason the house escaped the outcome of the Civil War unscathed, apart from the loss of its main tower, was that, while Sir Gilbert was a staunch Royalist, his son Richard who succeeded in 1648 was an equally devoted Parliamentarian!

As the Sealed Knot's members prepared for the fray, the village pubs were packed, Royalists in one, Roundheads in the other. Several hundred pints of bitter were raised to King Charles, Oliver Cromwell and other – to the general public – more obscure personages. Rousing songs were sung to the music of fife and drum, before it was on with the buckler and helmet and off up the hill. Sir Bernard, in full Cavalier outfit, played the part of his ancestor Sir Gilbert. He appeared in the courtyard for a pre-battle conference with his 'officers'. Seemingly satisfied with strategy, he mounted a suitably trained horse and sallied forth.

Sir Bernard de Hoghton, fourteenth baronet; *right*: as 'Sir Gilbert' before the 'battle' in 1978

Over the next couple of hours a crowd of some two thousand was entertained by an almost equally large crowd of pikemen, musketeers and camp followers. Cannon roared, 'blood' flowed, and ladies of doubtful virtue robbed the 'dead' of their valuables, while other more upright ladies were all but robbed of their virtue. Most of the afternoon's events related to the Battle of West Houghton (translated to a field below the tilting green from which the tenant's sheep had been evacuated for the day), naturally enough since this was a win for the Royalists and Sir Gilbert. At the end of the battle Sir Bernard good humouredly undertook his party piece, the acceptance of surrender by the defeated Parliamentarian forces in a march past of all those taking part.

The day's takings had been disappointing, but Sir Bernard was feeling philosophical: 'The Tower is like a good woman. You know you love her and yet you're driven mad by her. I see my efforts here today as a challenge, and the de Hoghtons have always risen to challenge.'

Ashington

Most of aall man 'twas the closeness of friends
Aroond us that helped us to bear
The many discomforts that Poverty sends,
For of these nearly aall had theor share . . .

Bill Coombs, a retired miner, searches in his poem for good things to say about the Ashington he remembers from his youth. What compliments there are go to the people, for their closeness, their neighbourliness, their community spirit, inevitable perhaps in a place that was and still is to the casual visitor, so visually unattractive.

Described in 1930 as the largest pit village in Europe, Ashington had grown from next to nothing in seventy years. In 1860 the population of the village of Fell 'em Doon was seventy-six, but by 1911 on the same site there was a boom town, a Dodge City of nearly twenty-five thousand. Before 1860, there had been no natural reason for a town on this windswept plateau with its flank to the North Sea, no major river crossing, no junction of trade routes or of valleys such as initiated settlements elsewhere. Then engineers found deep, thick seams of industrial coal, and the entrepreneurs followed close on their heels. This bonanza brought immigrants from the Scottish borders, from Ireland, and all over England, from places where hard times were taking their toll. Apart from the Irish driven out by the potato famines and farmers deserting the mean border lands between Ashington and the Forth, there were many from depressed trades related to mining, Cornish tin miners, Cumbrian lead miners, and quarrymen from Derbyshire and Dorset. This mixture of uprooted people poured in to fill the long terraces laid out by the mine owners like rifle barrels in a box. Then, as now, Ashington and its people adjusted to each other philosophically, and rapidly.

Today the population has levelled out at twenty-eight thousand, but although there is now a big aluminium smelter, a sizeable power station and an industrial estate on the outskirts of town, coal remains by far the biggest employer. Almost symbolically in this town without

High Market, Ashington, *c.* 1890

a steeple, the highest point is still the pithead gear. So there remains a cohesion to Ashington, and an attractiveness to the locals which largely eludes the outsider. Quality of life, they would argue, is not in material surroundings, but in people and in the shared experiences of a mining community.

Typical of 'Ashington lads' is Sammy Scott, now General Secretary of the Northumberland Miners' Union. Like his father he has done his time at most underground jobs at Ashington Colliery, as face worker, development worker opening up new seams, and as stone man separating stone from the coal, building roadways and putting up roof girders. Today his job is very different, much of his time being spent behind an enormous Victorian desk in central Newcastle. He works from the elegant surroundings of Burt Hall, the miners' headquarters built in the great days of 1895 and named after one of Sam's predecessors. Since the 1920s all the Union's general secretaries have been Ashington men, reflecting the pride of place the Ashington group of collieries has always held at the centre of the Northumbrian coalfield. At the end of each day with an almost audible sigh of relief, Sammy clears his desk and drives the seventeen miles back through the fields and woods to 'canny Ashington'. His family were immigrants to the boom town in the 1880s who had originally come down from the Cheviots only a dozen miles from the Scottish border. It is on record that the Scotts, along with families like the Humes and the Herons, had a reputation for riding close to the wind with other people's horses and cattle, but whether Sammy's own forebears were actually Border 'reivers', or more plainly cattle thieves, would be difficult to prove, or to disprove! Records of working men are scanty, and Scott is a common name in the Borders. We did establish that his great-grandfather John Scott had worked as a quarryman in Doddington, once a thriving market centre, but now little more than a huddle of farms around a tiny church and a ruined peel tower. Hard times forced John Scott to make the first move south to the ancient market town of Alnwick, where his son George Dunn Scott, Sammy's grandfather, eventually set up as a blacksmith. It was he who moved the family into the stone-and-cement rows thrown up alongside Ashington's first pit, operating a horse-and-cart business by day and supplementing the family income with a night shift down the mine.

Sammy, now a vigorous fifty-eight, sees himself as a product of that strong, hard-working tradition: 'My father was a stone man most of his working days. It was heavy work and he was a very small fellow – seven stone wet through as they say. Still, he could hold his own with any man at any job down the pit. I was the same, but there's a bit more of me!'

Now that he has a desk job he needs to keep an eye on his weight and general fitness, so in his lunch hours (another new experience for a miner), he jogs across the road to the municipal Turkish baths as part of a deliberate keep fit programme, a problem the working miner scarcely needs to consider: 'When he could, a miner had to build himself up for his work by eating a lot. I regularly used to eat breakfast, dinner, evening meal and supper because I was able to get rid of the surplus flesh at my work. Now I have to watch what I'm doing. Mind you, in my early days my basic meal down the mine was a couple or three slices of jam and bread and a bottle of water.'

One place where the Ashington miner's fitness has always shown up is on the football field. In 1951 Sammy was playing centre-forward for the town's team when they made the third round of the F.A. cup. That was no mean feat in a community that produced the famous footballers Bobby and Jack Charlton, and Jackie Milburn, even

Ashington Football Club in 1955. Sammy Scott is in the front row, second from left

though every boy did learn to play by kicking a ball endlessly round the patches of grass between the houses.

Sammy's best memories of the town are as it was in the new boom time which came to Ashington after the Second World War: 'When I came back from the Army in 1947 the place was a hive of industry. The collieries were going full steam ahead and employment was to the full. The streets were full of people and the picture houses were always chock-a-block. We were a self-sufficient community and we used to think there was no place in the world like Ashington. In fact it's still the only place for me and my family. When I've been away to conferences or even to other countries, as soon as I come north through that Tyne tunnel to the Northumberland side, I start singing!'

The sense of pride in a place which scarcely existed just over a century ago is equally pronounced, almost fierce, in those a generation older – even though many of them only came here in their youth from widely different backgrounds, when Ashington still had the air of a frontier town. In the smart parlour of Ross Miles' terraced house where strings of wagons constantly pass the window, empty in one direction, full the other, five such retired mineworkers of around seventy matched up their memories for us.

Larry Lavelle's father came to the area as a boy from County Mayo on the west coast of Ireland, so the concept of life as a struggle was nothing new: 'As I remember it as a young lad, times were very hard in Ashington in the twenties. My dad often went to the face with no "bait" in his tin. All the food he could afford went to bring up me and my four brothers.' The growth of the unions and the solidarity of the men behind Sammy Scott and the union today, he sees as inevitable: 'We had to have somebody to look after us. All the owners wanted was their pound of flesh – and I'm being as discreet as I can here. If you made one mistake you were out on your neck, and men were fighting for a job, any job, your job. With the old coal owners you weren't allowed an opinion – one mistake and you were out, boy.'

Old wounds like these heal slowly. Although more than thirty years have passed since the National Coal Board took over from the mine owners, there is still a hint of the 'master and man' atmosphere in the stiff formality when Sammy Scott and the local union men meet colliery officials in the mahogany-panelled offices at the pit.

Although Larry Lavelle only moved round the table to become a colliery official in his later working years under the Coal Board, Joe Ward had known what it was like to be one of the 'bosses' men' since he was twenty-two. He was born in Ashington after his family, who were professional people on Tyneside, had fallen on difficult times. Obviously there was still enough push in the family to get Joe through an apprenticeship as an electrician, but his memories of the twenties suggest that colliery officials were equally crushed by the realities of winning coal as a livelihood: 'The owners had a commandment: "The pit shall not stand!" So we were what we called "slaves of the lamp!" Even in the middle of the night if anything went wrong, an official had to get up and get there. You got hardened to it, mind.'

As with memories of any harsh life, the moments of escape stay bright. Ashington had after all been dropped like a field of volcanic lava into green and pleasant agricultural land, so Joe Ward's delights in the times that were his own are as rural as those of miners everywhere: 'On Sundays we'd get away for a country walk to places like Cresswell or Newbiggin-by-the-sea, or Woodhorn and Bedling-ton, and attend the church for a good sing – not for the religion. Then afterwards we'd go along to the pub for a drink. You see, most of the coal owners were teetotal, Quakers a lot of them, so originally Ashington was teetotal, and to get away at the weekend meant you could have a drink. I've known men walk miles during the working week to bring back beer from Sheepwash and places. Then the coal company started a sports club. For tuppence a week the youngsters could play cricket, tennis, football, hockey and there was boxing, ping pong and billiards. But I used to like camping. Right back in 1924 half a dozen of us had a camp near Cresswell, and during the General Strike we spent nearly all our time down there. The camping lasted right up to the beginning of the war, until we all got married!'

Ross Miles's people, like Sammy Scott's, came from the Border country, though a little further north, in the Scottish lowlands. At the time Ross's grandfather moved down to work on a farm near Ashington, the family were still all agricultural workers, and the association with the mines began only when his grandfather took the job of looking after food for the pit ponies. Ross spent most of his working life as an Ashington Coal Company official, and he was anxious to dispel any idea that *everything* was bad about a town with one industry and one boss: 'After all, the Ashington Coal Company built the place. They subsidised the building of everything cultural about the town – schools, workers' institutes, even churches. They even supported the co-operative movement by being members of the Ashington Industrial Co-op. Then, they gave their employees the opportunity to own their own houses. This house we live in now was built for about £480 in the early twenties, and when the scheme started in 1924, all I had to do was put down a £5 deposit and then pay ten bob a week which was stopped off my pay.'

Pat Brannigan, of Irish descent like Larry Lavelle, had listened to both sides of the argument. He came in his twenties from the then depressed Cramlington area of the Northumberland coalfield to Ashington where the owners were acknowledged to be better employers: 'But they were still not *good* employers; they still demanded their pound of flesh. The basic truth was that they did not pay the men that produced the coal properly; all they were after was profits. Ashington may have had the widest front street of any mining area, with shops down either side, but you still had to go knee-deep in mud across the backs to the toilet.'

The dirt was offensive to what Pat remembers as 'clean-living people'. Even so, Ashington was the last colliery in the area to have pithead baths. The miners themselves opposed them on the principle that their wives needed a bath just as much as they did, and they would rather the coal owners added a bathroom to their homes than provide baths at the pithead! Many face workers, though, actually believed that washing the back would weaken it. As a boy, Pat Brannigan saw the shield of dirt on his father's back every night as he washed in the big tin bath by the fire. Sitting next to Pat, Bill Coombs surprised even his contemporaries by pointing out that he himself had worked for three years at the face before he first washed his back at the age of eighteen. His great-grandfather had first come to the area as a London seaman on the coal boats to the Tyne, and Bill's grandfather, his father, and Bill himself, worked all their adult lives down the pit.

Today the workers' educational institutes set up by the paternalistic coal owners are derelict or gone, but many of those owners would smile in their Quaker graves at the achievements of some Ashington miners. Bill Coombs is setting down his as yet unpublished memoirs in a growing collection of evocative verse. At seventy-four, artist Oliver Kilbourn is still painting lovingly his memories of the coalface, the pit ponies and even the red and gold smoking pitheaps that have now been levelled. He and the Ashington Group of painters have established an international reputation through their canvases of such apparently prosaic subjects as a chip shop, a street corner or a union meeting. The same warmth of social life characterises Bill Coombs' poetry, but always by contrast with the pit he had escaped from:

> And huw did we dee at the end of the week
> When wor pay barely met wor expense man?
> And lux'ries were plisures that thrilled us to seek
> But cost at the most a few pence man.

> We spent wor spare time, when we finished wor chores,
> In the fields and the woods, happy oors man,
> Developin' friendships and luv of ootdoors
> 'Mang the bords and the trees and the flooers man.

> But most of aall man 'twas the closeness of friends
> Aroond us that helped us to bear
> The many discomforts that Poverty sends,
> For of these nearly aall had theor share.

And still theor were gud things in life, be it said,
Forbye its mare unpleasant labours,
Consarn for yor welfare, material aid,
Were riches enjoyed b' gud naybours.

Poverty is undeniably a rare experience today, but such continuity of work keeps memories fresh, and 'unpleasant labours' are by no means a thing of the past. Conditions generally may be vastly improved, but it is as well to remember as you walk the broad main street of Ashington that not far away there are still men underground, cramped in narrow, wet seams, working coal with picks.

Although Sammy Scott will readily admit that he is fighting now for much less basic things than in the past, he sees the role of the union today in terms as aggressive as ever. He is thankful that his predecessors got rid of injustices like the Bond, which tied a man to his pit like a slave for twelve months. Gone too are the mine owner's 'tommy shops' – the only place where the pitman could spend the tokens with which he was paid – and the 'candymen' who evicted families of miners who were unable to fulfil the terms of their 'bond' even if only through sickness. But to a man who, as a child, saw a family being thrown out of their house, even the allocation of Coal Board houses to face workers only is an affront. So his struggle goes on – for better protective clothing, for a total end to pick and shovel working in narrow seams, and eventually for a four-day week. He insists that the nature of the job itself has never changed: 'The miner has to fight the elements in the geological conditions underground just as the deep sea fisherman has to fight the elements at sea. This accounts for the comradeship, and for the one great thing that we have in the mining industry – our solidarity. Once you go down that mine it gets in your bloodstream, and that's what makes me proud to be following on in the tradition of people like Martin Jude and Tom Burt who led our earlier struggles.' It seems strange to hear these sentiments coming from such a relaxed character in a smart business suit.

The collective spirit that shows itself in the Union is seen even more vividly in the social atmosphere of that most Geordie of all Ashington's institutions, the workingmen's club. The town still boasts twenty-three such clubs for a population of twenty-eight thousand. Many were set up in the late nineteenth-century by the miners as educational and debating centres for the self-improvement

Saturday night at the Club – a painting by Oliver Kilbourn in the 1930s

of the mining community. To that extent they paralleled the institutes
set up by the owners, facilities which even then many working men
regarded with suspicion as paternalistic and too closely supervised.
Bosses like the teetotal Quaker Priestman, who was Managing Director of the Ashington Coal Company, wanted the workers to live their
lives 'in all sobriety, honesty and with due diligence towards honour-
able toil and the gains to be had therefrom.' The clubs began as
islands of escape for the workers from such paternalistic attitudes, but
it was not until 1892 – after Priestman's death – that the coal owners
set up the first *licensed* premises in Ashington. This was the Portland
Hotel, built as a respectable place to dine or to stay when they or their
business guests came to visit the colliery. As attitudes to drink
relaxed, the clubs too began to sell strong drink to their members.
Membership was a gesture of identity, almost of defiance, which
meant that public houses never really gained a foothold in Ashington.
The only other pub in Ashington apart from the Portland and the
Grand is still known locally as 'The White Elephant'!

Outside, the clubs' names in vivid neon remind you of their origin, the 'Constitutional', the 'Industrial', the 'Comrades', the 'Excelsior' whose mock-Greek portals were once the exclusive haunt of overmen and under managers. Inside though, the clubs reflect the society of a wider world. Top pop groups are paid the going rate and play to packed houses of well-dressed young men and women who can afford up to £5 admission and the scampi and chips. The older generation have their well-attended Old Tyme dancing nights, or their 'Go as you please' when anyone is encouraged to get up and give a song, do a dance, tell a few jokes, or in the vernacular 'Shar their motions'. These days scant attention is paid to the works of Ruskin and John Stuart Mill, still ranged in dusty glass cabinets in the upper rooms of a few clubs. Although one club still presents the generally unacceptable face of male chauvinism with a sign 'No Ladies Allowed' on its front door (universal in the past), in most clubs the womenfolk are now an accepted part of the evening get-togethers. The present Scott clan for example, Sammy and his sons Ray and David and their wives will share an evening's entertainment over a few drinks either in Sammy's club, the Comrades, or Ray and David's, the New Northern.

Sammy's sons have both married local girls, though neither of them are miners' daughters. In Sammy's young days virtually all the pit lads married girls from mining families too, but although the coming of other industries has made that less likely, both his sons' wives have accepted the traditions and attractions of a mining community that make the Scott menfolk describe Ashington as 'the only place in the world'. These days tradition does not necessarily demand that son follows father down the pit too, but many sons still look to the pit, as young men in other parts might look to the Army, as a place to acquire 'a trade'.

Both Sammy's sons took his advice and served an apprenticeship at the pit. One stayed, the other left, a difference which shows in each of them separate aspects of the family make-up. David, just under thirty, is not tall, and is sparely built, but like his father known as an aggressive performer on the football field. He plays regularly for the New Northern Club team – the self-improving libraries may have gone, but sports activities are still very much associated with the clubs. David is well settled in as an electrician at Ellington Colliery, one of the pits in the Ashington group and the pit where his father worked. He seems positively at home as he strides, black-faced, across the pit-yard, hangs up his lamp, strips off and joins his hundred or so workmates in the communal showers, all of them naked except for coal dust and the inevitable blue scars on hands and faces.

Ray Scott is a couple of years older than his brother, and, according to his father, a throwback to Sammy's grandfather, the blacksmith-turned-waggoner. Ray is extrovert, with heavy sideburns and a generous build like his father. He has exchanged his job as a colliery mechanic for a freer existence as dealer, gardener, pig rearer and purveyor of most things. On his allotment he keeps rabbits and a few turkeys as well as pigs, he grows tomatoes, cuts up firewood and buys and sells a few old cars for scrap. In his house at Newbiggin, a seaside colliery village, there are guns and crossbows on the wall, ferrets in the garden shed. Ray represents the enterprise in the Scott clan which goes back to Border days. Naturally enough then, he is the one to take time off and support his father in a pilgrimage back to the Northern haunts of the Scotts.

Every Shrove Tuesday since time out of mind, Alnwick has been the setting for a strange game of football. In its early days the match was played through the narrow main street of Alnwick, but the increasing chaos and damage caused the Duke of Northumberland to move it in 1828 out to his pastures in the shadow of Alnwick Castle. Since 1847 the game has been played on the present pasture, the North Desmesne. It starts with the ball being thrown down from the castle's gatehouse by the Duke's representative. In February 1978 Ray and Sammy Scott were among the crowd that followed the Duke's piper over the bridge past the straight-tailed Percy family lion on to the field of play, a boggy meadow a quarter of a mile long. Since the 1860s the game has been formalised as a match between the two parishes of St Michael and St Paul, but it hardly seemed to matter on which side Sammy should join in the game on behalf of his forebears. The winner is the first side to score two goals, or 'hales', by kicking the ball between the leafy bowers that form the goal posts. Such challenges in the Border reiving days between, say, the Robsons and the Armstrongs might well have finished up in bloodshed, but nowadays Sammy and the older hands retire to the bar of the Oddfellows Arms to dry out and tuck into tea and sandwiches. They leave today's young blades to jump in the river after the ball. Tradition has it that the first to carry the ball out to the other bank can keep it, an honour well-earned in the middle of February!

Shrove Tuesday football at Alnwick

It is easy to see what Ashington means to people like the Scott family with their roots in the land as well as the pit, but it may be more difficult to understand what the younger generation see in Ashington or coal-mining. At the Ashington colliery area training school, where trainee face workers learn how to erect pit-props for their own safety, and how to deal with the fearsome-toothed coal-cutting machines, we talked to some of the young miners. Two local lads, Alec Sellars and Harry Elliott from Blyth, once a thriving coal port, stressed both the matiness and the money. To Ray Common from Ashington itself it was a harsh fact of life that mining offered security to a family man but, remembering the many operations his father suffered as a result of dust on the lungs, he wished he could see a paying alternative.

The fourth young miner we talked to, Russell Waldie, was a young Scot from the same Border country that Sammy Scott's ancestors had left: 'I came basically for security. I'm a joiner by trade, but I was sick of moving around, fighting every day for my money. You can't build a good family life around circumstances like that. Here you can't help but like the surroundings, and your mates. They're laughing and

Trainee miners and instructor on the mock coal face at Ashington Colliery

joking all day – even when they're upset and arguing, there's still something to smile about.' Strong echoes of Ashington's earlier days, rough and ready, but very warm and very human.

Russell's parents tried to put him off mining because of the dangers, but the terrible injuries men suffered with monotonous regularity in the past obviously occur less frequently now. When such accidents do happen, sophisticated treatment and long-term rehabilitation care are always available at the expense of the state. One such rehabilitation centre was established in the 1950s at Hartford Hall, near Ashington, a gracious mansion built for one Squire Burden of Bedlington, a mine owner. Sammy Scott and his Union President Denis Murphy no doubt smile at the thought of Squire Burden's reaction as they sit and watch disabled miners running three-legged races across his front lawns at their annual sports day.

By far the biggest annual event in the community calendar is the Miners' Picnic, a close relation to the Durham Miners' Gala in the

Pithead gear at Ashington Colliery

neighbouring coalfield. It is held one Saturday in June through the streets and in the fields of Bedlington, a few miles away from Ashington. One year the Picnic was held, disastrously, in Ashington itself. It was a flop. Somehow transferring it to Bedlington makes it feel more like a day out, and even hardier upholders of Ashington's merits concede that the greener banks and fields of Bedlington make a better setting for a summer happening. The tradition dates back to 1866 when the miners of Northumberland gathered at Polly's Folly to hear their leaders. Since then the gathering has lapsed only during the two World Wars, and now what Sammy Scott calls 'wor day', draws miners' representatives from all over the country, as well as many Ashingtonians who today have nothing to do with the pit.

The day begins very early. Before eight o'clock a fleet of double decker buses pulls into Bedlington's main car park. The brass bands that emerge have already woken up their own towns and villages with a march through the streets soon after seven, and now, one after

Sammy and friends at the Miners' Picnic, Bedlington

another, they assemble their lodge banners and raise them in the bright morning air. The Ashington Colliery Band with Sammy Scott at its head moves off to treat the sleepy citizens of Bedlington to the full brazen blast of 'Slaidburn', the hymn tune in minor key that, played by a miners' band manages to convey both a memory of hard times and an air of defiance. On the surface the Picnic is a casual affair, but through the day it runs with a military precision. The pubs open at nine o'clock mainly, it is alleged, for the refreshment of bandsmen who by now are practising in every pub yard for their band contest that begins precisely at 9.30am. The contest takes place in the middle of the main street where, one by one, the bands march into position and perform in front of an open upstairs window where the judge sits, back turned, and marks each band, identified to him only by a number. Later, huddles of bandsmen sit around outside the pubs, listening intensely to friends' cassette recordings of their performance. They will have to wait for the judge's verdict until the end of the afternoon after the political speeches.

The front row of the procession is as powerful a line-up of left wing talent as one could expect to see anywhere. In 1978 Tony Benn and Judith Hart, then ministers in the Labour Government, together with Lawrence Daly, Secretary of the National Union of Mineworkers, marched alongside Sammy Scott in front of the bands and banners. The Picnic is a children's day too, and they are represented in the procession by the twenty-odd juvenile jazz bands with their kazoos and drums, each band in its own uniform of brightly-coloured home-made costumes. They are a reminder of the days when everyone made their own entertainment with the cheapest instruments possible, and dressed up in bright colours as a cheering contrast with drab surroundings. As the procession moved into the meadow for the speeches, a voice in the crowd shouted 'Howway wor side!' In some quarters at least the class war is not yet over.

The platform party were given a long welcome by the crowd of thousands. Sammy Scott and Denis Murphy cracked a few jokes, and welcomed a Polish delegation. Then Judith Hart was introduced, and she put in a nutshell what the crowd wanted to hear, what the day meant to them: 'When one has something like the Northumberland Miners' Picnic . . . you feel that the meaningfulness and the solidarity of the working-class and the labour movement of this country is something beyond recognition. And it brings a warmth to your heart, and it brings, if you like, a rekindling of the sense of purpose. And I envy you the warmth and enthusiasm of this day in Bedlington.'

The formal part of the day ended at about half-past four, as the platform party departed to Netherton Social Club for high tea. The Ashington band had won the contest for the eleventh, or was it the twelfth, year running. Yet another Picnic had run smoothly, and no doubt Sammy and Denis would be back in the Comrades Club for a well-earned pint before the night was out. Once again it had been a day of traditional celebration, almost ritual, which lends an air of permanence to Ashington and its major industry.

But the possibility of change has crossed the mind of newcomers like the young Scot, Russell Waldie: 'I've started to build myself a new life here, and I'd be very disappointed to have to move. I keep my fingers crossed that the coalfields in this area will see me to my retiring age.'

The Miners' Picnic is as durable as the coalfields themselves, evidence of a continuity that would only be broken if the unthinkable happened – if the coal ran out.

Whitby

Fare thee well my canny lass
Farewell Whitby Town,
For I'm going away on a tall ship
To hunt the whale fish down.

To hear a North Yorkshire folk group singing that song to the accompaniment of an accordion conjures up a vision of Whitby's harbourside as it might have been in the bright but misty light of an April morning two hundred years ago. A crowd of men, women and children hovers excitedly near the end of the quay, their attention focused on a ship similar to those favoured by Captain Cook for his voyages round the world. It is packed with stores and at its mainmast head hangs a garland of flowers and ribbons. Then a figure appears and the crowds part to let him through to the gangplank. This is Captain William Scoresby, a bull of a man, Whitby's greatest whaling captain who made some thirty voyages to the Arctic and £90,000 profit for himself and his partners. The women watch as the ropes are cast off and the vessel slips out of the harbour. It is the start of a voyage to the Arctic whaling grounds, and for the men aboard a five-month-struggle exposed to danger, and the daily risk of death.

No one hunts whales out of Whitby today, but fishing is still its lifeblood, still the town's key enterprise. The steep streets lead down to the river Esk, a straight waterway running from the now disused Whitehall Shipyard, where Cook's ships were built, out through the narrow harbour entrance into the wild North Sea. Traffic winds its way around the town and over the ancient swing bridge as best it can. In the old town the houses all seem to have angled themselves slightly towards the sea with scarcely a glance over their shoulders up-river. Once it was known as Streonshalh and Saxons kept watch from the west cliff for Viking raiders, for the town has always looked outward to the North Sea for its living and its highway. On the landward side Whitby turns its back on a rampart of moorland – the first decent road over these moors was built little more than a hundred years ago.

Whitby harbour and town – a view from St Mary's Church towards West Cliff

Even today it takes little in the way of winter snowfall for Whitby to be cut off from the rest of England.

The sea too is violent and unpredictable, and Whitby is the only harbour for miles along one of the most treacherous coastlines in Britain. Before the days of navigational aids and powerful, reliable engines, sailing ships faced with stormy weather were in a terrible dilemma, whether to aim for the narrow harbour entrance or try to sail around the rocky promontory to the north. In the sudden gales which blow in from the north-east literally hundreds of ships came to grief along this unbroken stretch of cliffs, headlands and underwater reefs. It was in these circumstances that the rowing lifeboats of Whitby became famous. The pay was an incentive, but the boats the men rowed would scarcely inspire confidence today, though the *Robert and Ellen Robson* was taken out of service only in 1957, the last rowing boat in the Royal National Lifeboat Institution's fleet. Throughout their history from 1802 until quite recently, the two Whitby lifeboats were

Lifeboat disaster in 1861: engraving from the *Illustrated London News*

manned predominantly by fishermen. The risks were great and many lives were lost, as gravestones in St Mary's churchyard on East Cliff testify.

The gravestones of John and William Storr on the cliff edge itself overlook the scene of Whitby's worst lifeboat disaster. On 9 February 1861 a great North-easterly gale drove a total of eight ships on to the beaches around Whitby. The lifeboat was launched four times and brought twenty-five men to safety, then put off again to a schooner foundering no more than forty yards from the pier. A freak wave overturned the lifeboat, and eleven of the twelve crewmen were drowned within sight of their own homes and a helpless crowd on the pier. In the flagstoned porch of St Mary's church a marble memorial records the fishermen whose family names still form the backbone of the quayside fraternity today, names like Leadley, Harland and Storr.

The name Storr is pure Norse, and is recorded in Whitby as early as 1620. Thomas Storr, brother of John and William, survived only

Fishing boats at Whitby – one of Frank Meadow Sutcliffe's nineteenth-century photographs

because after two trips in the lifeboat he had been called away to rescue his own fishing coble which had slipped its moorings. The two main branches of the Storr family in Whitby today owe their existence to that happy accident. Late in life Thomas was photographed by the famous Whitby photographer Frank Meadow Sutcliffe, and on his knee is a three-year-old boy destined to become another Whitby legend, his grandson John Robert 'Dandy' Storr.

'Dandy' Storr, in recent times the patriarch of the family, died in 1968 at his home in Church Street on the eve of his eighty-eighth birthday. He had begun fishing in 1893 and was one of the first Whitby men to own a deep-sea keel-boat which, in accordance with his very strong religious principles, he called *Pilot Me*. It was his habit to sing Sankey revivalist hymns at the wheel as the boat ploughed through heavy seas to the fishing grounds. His favourite was of course 'Jesus, Saviour, pilot me'. For many years until his death he was the acknowledged leader of the fishing community, and of his twenty-one children, four sons became skippers of fishing boats.

Dandy's son George followed in his father's footsteps as church-

Morning and evening – Thomas Storr with his grandson 'Dandy' on his knee

warden at St Mary's, climbing the hundred and ninety-nine steps twice a day to the East Cliff where a church has stood for thirteen centuries. Both he and his brother Matty are still in the choir at the Seamen's Mission and sing the same Sankey hymns as their father. Matty is retired from skippering now, but his small figure in large flat cap can be seen most mornings on the fish quay helping to unload the catch. Though he is not averse to taking a bottle or two of Jubilee Stout these days in the Marine Hotel after choir practice, he still tells with pride and humour stories about his father's day: 'We went straight to sea from school, straight on board. My father was tough but fair – you had to do everything he told you at the double. I was sick for the first six months, my brother for twelve months! A lot of them would be sick on Monday mornings after a weekend on the drink, but none of us used to smoke or drink – we couldn't afford to.'

With 'Dandy' Storr smoking and drinking were against his religion too, but these principles also had a marked effect on the way he and his sons approached fishing. Matty recalls: 'We never went on a Sunday; we always finished on a Saturday night. My father never went on a Sunday in his life, and that's more than any of us could say now. He also believed in not being greedy, in sharing the fish. That's why later on, when my brother and I went fishing as skippers, we wouldn't use the seine nets. They caught too many fish, so we felt it was against our conscience to use them. But we threw a lot of money away, make no mistake about it. J.J., my father's brother, his side of the family did very well with the seine net.'

But apart from the problems of his conscience Matty did not have the sons that are essential to this family-based industry: 'My oldest brother had a home-grown crew when he got his boat, but I didn't marry till late because all I thought about was football – I didn't believe in women. When I did get married, I had four girls first. Then one Christmas Eve I got a boy, I had one more go and I got another girl! That's really what finished me in the fishing line.'

The only time ashore to see the strength of the Whitby fishing community is on a Friday morning shortly after dawn. The quayside by the fish market rapidly fills up with brightly painted keel-boats bearing names like *Success*, *Wakeful*, *Venus*, and *Scoresby*, and (a reminder of Dandy Storr's day) *Lead Us*. The boats have been at sea since Sunday night, passing wary messages by radio telephone to their agents ashore about their catch and position, messages that may often be more misleading than helpful because everyone (including their wives) listens to the radio telephone. They may have been in once during the week with a particularly good catch either here or, if they heard the prices were better, to one of the other East coast ports such as Grimsby, but now they are all home and with the market rule of 'first landed, first sold' there is fierce competition to get the catch ashore. Young lads in sea boots with tartan mufflers knotted at their throats leap ashore and make fast, and for a couple of hours there is hectic activity as the boxes are landed, weighed and stacked, ready for the auctioneer. When his performance is through, it is time for fishermen of all generations to take their ease in the half-dozen pubs along the quay.

Perhaps the favourite, though it also has the advantage of being the nearest, is the 'Pier' where old Jake Cole walks round dishing out the weekly wage packets. These days some skippers prefer to pay their men by cheque to encourage the young to save, but, cash or cheque, Whitby still operates the 'share system'. The owner (usually the skipper) takes fifty per cent of the income from the catch for running costs and expenses, then distributes the rest in equal pay packets to all the crew, apart from apprentices still learning the trade, who get a half or three-quarter share for the first year or two. As the pub fills up, Jake, an enormous man with gravel voice and twinkling eyes, loosens his collar and settles down to his 'drop of medicine', a large gin and tonic. Across the bar his son John plays dominoes with Billy Storr, one of J. J. Storr's successful sons, small and dark with deep-set eyes like many of the family. This is the start of the 'fisherman's weekend'. As Billy Storr puts it: 'We work hard out there, and long hours, sometimes for nowt. So Friday we have a few pints and a bit of real sleep, same on Saturday. Then Sunday night between ten and midnight it's back to sea for the week.' And though many fishermen may be heavy drinkers at the weekend, no booze goes with them to sea. This is one job where sobriety at work may still mean the difference between life and death.

Most of Whitby's keel-boats are still family owned and operated, but with rapidly rising costs the replacement of older boats is making family ownership more and more difficult. Jim Leadley has two boats, *Success I* and *Success II*; leaving his two sons to take out *Success II*, he runs the older boat himself. Twenty years ago *Success I* cost him

£14,000, but now it would cost in the region of £250,000 to replace. Even the deposit would frighten off most families today.

William Hall, the youngest of Whitby's keel-boat skippers, has had to persuade a local fish-selling company to put their trust in him and provide him with a boat: 'My father didn't have a boat, he was just an ordinary fisherman, so I worked my way up from being a deck-hand because I wanted to better myself. You have to learn how to do everything though – it's no good going aboard as skipper, standing in the wheelhouse and telling them how to do a job if you can't do it yourself. But now I'm a skipper, there's no way I'd be able to put down £60,000 for a boat of my own, it's an impossibility. It's a lot of money for such as Jim and his family who've been working at it all their lives, especially when you think you've got to make about £600 a week to cover expenses before you take anything home.'

Jake Cole is now near the end of his fishing career and his two sons are already well-established aboard the family boat *Venus*. Like his sons he was brought up to the job and knew nothing else, but he is pessimistic about the future for those whose fathers do not have boats, including the fifteen per cent who are unemployed in Whitby each winter. A government scheme to subsidise local lads as apprentices aboard the boats was scarcely discussed before it fizzled out, though on the face of it the skippers were enthusiastic. Jake said: 'The idea was that we'd put them on to a small share basis, and if they took to the job, we'd keep them on. There are plenty of young lads knocking about that want to go fishing, and this would get them a livelihood.'

Tal Bennison though, skipper of *Scoresby* and successful enough to be awaiting delivery of a new £200,000 boat when we talked to him, is realist enough to see another problem about such an apprentice scheme: 'Well, it would fetch new blood into the trade, but whether the lads would ever adapt to it I don't know. If you were brought up to a job like we were, it comes natural to you, but it's hard to ask young lads to come from being farmhands, for instance, to this. The normal working week can be anything up to a hundred hours, and very few people can work so long. A man working ashore with those hours would expect to do well, but for a hundred hours at sea you could go home with nothing. It all depends on the price of the fish, how many fish you catch, and if you catch no fish, you get no money.'

Jake Cole puts it simply: 'To be a proper inshore fisherman, you must take your good times with your bad. You get these cowboys coming into it and they go for a week or two, catch nothing, and they're running up that road – they've seen enough of fishing!'

Now that their keel-boats are bristling with navigational aids and fish-finding devices, it might be expected that such lean times would have been eliminated for the professionals, but fishermen will always be dependent on the weather, and even in recent years stormy winters have often meant poor catches. The other skippers nod in vigorous agreement when Billy Storr reminds them of 1947: 'I was fishing with my father then, potting, and we went two months without making anything at all. Nothing.'

No matter how bad the worst years though, the Whitby men are loath to see themselves under the protective umbrella of a big trawler company. Put in general terms they will accept the suggestion that the next decade or two will see a continuing trend towards the bigger companies and away from the family concerns, but any suggestion that the established skippers, or their sons with access to boats would work for these companies, is dismissed instantly. Billy Storr expresses the strong streak of independence in all of them: 'Say, for instance, we went to Grimsby, where most boats are run by big companies. There *they* tell *you* when to sail. With any of us *we* say when we're going and we come back when we're ready. No boss tells us, but with the trawler companies they tell you when to come into port and when to go out, no matter what the weather. The skipper doesn't decide, and there's no way any of our crews would stand for that.'

Threatening to go and work on the trawlers out of Grimsby is one method used by Whitby sons to persuade reluctant fathers to take them aboard the fishing boats, and usually such a show of determination works, as it did for Jim Leadley's son, young Jim. Now most of those in the know on the quayside will tell you that the Leadleys' boats more than live up to their name *Success*.

In spite of his initial reluctance to see his sons in fishing, Jim agrees with Tal Bennison about the difficulties of bringing in 'outsiders' because of the long hours and a social life crowded into forty-eight hours at the weekend, but he also sees a problem in the responsibilities involved: 'It is one of the snags of the share system that a very young chap can earn very big money before he's used to it. Then he gets his slack weeks with no money at all; but some weeks he does get very big money and some of them haven't the temperament to handle it. They go off the rails. You must remember that when one of the chaps comes

Matty Storr, Jim Leadley and Bob Harland aboard *Success II*

to be skipper he has the lives of five men in his hands; he takes a boat probably worth £250,000 to sea. He's got to make that pay, and he's got to earn a living for five men entirely off his own bat. A lot of them just won't have the responsibility and, believe me, it is a big responsibility, especially for a young chap.'

But with unemployment high in Whitby, manpower, Jim believes, is not fishing's biggest problem. Until the middle of 1979 he was active in the National Federation of Fishermen's Organisations, and particularly in the Anglo-Scottish Fish Producers' Organisation which monitors fishermen's interests within the E.E.C. Like all British fishermen Jim Leadley wants government action to secure a better common fishing policy inside the Common Market and he is constantly disappointed by the limited restrictions placed on foreign fleets, but he is also in no doubt as to the problems caused by policy closer home: 'You run into the usual snags with family businesses. You get a death in the family and that throws a huge spanner in the works, because you come in for death duties on your boats and, like everything else, it just smashes the whole thing up. In ten years' time you may get the odd family business, but unless government policy alters as regards death duties and grants and loans for boats, there's nothing can stop the big trawler owners becoming the biggest owners of inshore boats. Nothing at all.'

If the term 'inshore' sounds moderately comfortable, it is worth remembering that, as used by the Whitby keelboatmen, it means anything up to a hundred miles off into the North Sea. Not that the young would-be fisherman needs to go that far to discover that long hours and an unpredictable income are not the only drawbacks to the job. We joined the Leadleys on a trip to the fishing grounds and soon found out that even on a bright, crisp, May morning, the swell can be vigorous once you leave the protection of the twin stone piers at the mouth of the harbour. To anyone whose experience of sea-going vessels is limited to little more than stabilised cross-Channel ferries, the pitch and roll of the chunky little keelboat can at first be rather disconcerting. Even if you are not seasick, on deck you can be chilled to the bone within the first few miles of 'steaming' to the grounds. Then, after hours of inactivity, there is suddenly work to be done. With the boat on 'slow-ahead' the winches scream as a whole load of nets, floats and finger-cracking ironmongery go over the side, or as the fishermen put it, the trawl net is 'shot'.

While we trawled, Jim Leadley summed up the challenges: 'Before, fishing was purely a hunting game. You came out, caught what fish you could, came in and hoped for good markets. Now you've got to learn to live with regulations, quotas and a whole new set of market conditions. Everyone puts in far longer hours than they used to, but over against that a lot of the hard work has been taken out of it because these boats are pretty well fully-mechanised. But if you asked me what made a good fisherman, I'd still have to say experience, and if you really come down to it, sheer doggedness and cussedness that he won't be beat.' Jim Leadley has spent a lifetime weighing up these qualities. He is a big man himself and, like most of the Whitby skippers, has the red-rimmed, watery eyes that seldom sleep: 'I would say that the longest a man can go without sleep and be fully effective is about forty-eight hours. Beyond that, I reckon you could stay at the job up to one hundred hours with a minimum of an hour to an hour and a half's sleep out of twenty-four. But you must have some.' And even in these days of 'mechanised' fishing the onus is still on individual performance: 'We have to work our crews harder for the simple reason that the expenses and what-not have gone up so drastically that on each boat we are carrying at least one crew member less than we did eight years ago. We carry five now instead of six, and that's pretty general throughout the Whitby fleet.'

If the essential role of the fisherman has changed little, neither has that of the womenfolk. Their lot is still to wait and worry. Though these days they can listen in to their husbands' messages to shore on short-wave radio, the ever-present tension still mounts towards the end of the week. In the kitchen of their smart modern bungalow along the West Cliff, Jim Leadley's wife Alice and his mother Hilda, who lives next door, pause from gutting fish for the freezer. Hilda, a forthright and vigorous Yorkshirewoman, looks down at the table as she quietly illustrates the feelings of one who has a son and two grandsons at sea: 'I remember one day they'd all come in but ours. We only found out later they'd had to put in to Hartlepool. They'd had a bonny carry-on. The lifeboat from here was out for them, and we kept going and looking out for them, but anyway they survived. . .' They had stood on West Cliff, scene of the autumn watch by Whitby women who waited for a sight of the whalers returning from the north, hoping they would see the jawbone of a whale strapped to the mast, a sign that all aboard were safe and well. Neither of these women had wanted their men to go to sea, and it is not a problem that stops with the present working generation. Hilda pointed out forcibly that her grandson's two boys aged fifteen and eleven just cannot be kept away from the boats, so it seems her worries will never decrease.

Not all of Whitby's fishermen go off into deep water for days at a time. Increased specialisation has brought with it such a separation of activities and a division of interests that there are now two fishermen's associations, the Keelboatmen and the Coble Fishermen. Down past the swing bridge in the inner harbour along by the Angel Inn are the pretty little cobles that feature on so many Yorkshire calendars. Their owners are the true 'inshore' fishermen who go off the odd mile or two by the day to fish with pots, lines and fixed nets. While the family firms of keelboat men face up to the huge capital cost of maintaining independence from the big companies, the equally old-established coble fishing families grapple with the opposite problem of defending themselves from the 'little man', the part-timer. Because these smaller boats can be bought, or even hired, relatively cheaply and the necessary gear is none too expensive either (especially the easy-to-use trammel-net which simply hangs in the water from a series of floats), 'the butcher, the baker and the candlestick-maker' are increasingly muscling in on a patch of water that the coble men believe is already over-crowded. What annoys these self-employed fishermen even more is their firm belief that few of the part-timers ever tell the tax man about their activities!

One of the more picturesque cottages on Whitby's East Side often resounds to the protests of the coble men who meet under their secretary, Bob Harland, who has rebuilt and restored this house that he was born in. His great-great-great uncle died in the lifeboat disaster of 1861, and he himself won the R.N.L.I. silver medal in 1946. Now partly retired, Bob Harland is as much the elder statesman among the coble men as Jim Leadley is among the keelboat men, and he is quite explicit about the difference in their interests: 'The keelboat men are trawling, so they're not tied to any particular ground. They put the net over and pick it up maybe ten to fifteen miles away. As for us, our gear is static – we shoot it and it stays there. Most of the keelboat men try to keep clear of our gear, but some couldn't care less. They shut their eyes, and then you get all this hard feeling between us. But on the major issues we're together.' One of these is 'foreign intrusion': 'After all, it's our water, our sea. We've fished these grounds for centuries and now we're supposed to hand them over on a plate to the continentals! The way I look at it if the sea was farmed properly, if it was looked after, there'd be fish for everybody.'

For the most part Bob Harland, like Jim Leadley, is a modest, quiet chap, but in conversation it comes out that his experience too extends a bit beyond Whitby. He has looked at techniques in other parts of the world and on occasion has gone abroad himself in an advisory capacity. So the coble men listen to him as their spokesman: 'We want a coastal strip of three miles. That's what we need for conservation, and a lot of the keelboat men agree. Let me put it this way though. I fight for the young ones because they've laid out a lot of money, but I'm sorry to say it's true that I'd rather be at the end of a fishing career at the present time than at the beginning of one.'

The key problem in Whitby is employment, as there is no real alternative to fishing. It is a sign of the changing times that the famous Whitehall Shipyard where Captain Cook had his ships built, now functions only as a club and disco. Until recently, under a succession of 'incomer' owners it was building, for example, small steel-hulled inshore boats for such purposes as coastal protection in the Gulf States. Jim Leadley argues that, given a proper support policy with Whitby's interests foremost, it could function again and provide the town with a significant number of jobs, but for the moment it serves as a useful place to meet some of the younger fishermen having a few pints after a game of football. Even with their one-track minds about fishing as a livelihood, they had looked at the alternatives. The brightest hope seemed to be travelling to I.C.I. on Teesside, but that meant the unthinkable prospect of an hour each way to work by bus!

Boats are still built in Whitby in Jack Lowther's shipyard just under the bridge from the Whitehall Shipyard. Here, inside a big, bare shed, Jack and a few young lads turn out a steady supply of cobles constructed to an unwritten pattern the Vikings would have recognised. Beams of oak form the frame, and planks of larch the 'straked', or overlapped, cladding, each boat being custom built to meet the conditions of the East coast beach from which it will operate. But the apprenticeships are few, and the chosen are lucky.

The pressure is clearly on the fishing families to find work for their young men. At the height of his career as a keelboat skipper, forty-three-year-old Georgie Storr handed over the helm of the family boat *C.K.S.* (named after his children, Colin and Katherine) to blood three young lads aboard a tub named *Pat Marie*. His crew were Richard Storr, a cousin, Gibson Alley whose mother is a Storr, and Terry Naylor, the son of a quayside publican. Despite numerous setbacks with the newly-acquired 'extra' boat, including perpetual mechanical trouble, Georgie seemed to be teaching them the rudiments of trammel-netting. At the time we went to sea with them, Georgie complained they were 'not getting enough hours in to make a good living', but there was the strong impression that all three trainees were acquiring the chance of finding a keelboat berth in the future, where raw apprentices could no longer be considered.

Richard Storr was one of the determined young fishermen in their late teens and early twenties whom we met in the Shipyard Club. The family had literally made him a job, which contrasted strangely with the commonplace story among the group of paternal opposition to sons going 'to the fishing'. Richard's cousin, Barry Storr, told a typical story: 'I had to go and live with me Gran and Grandad to get fishing. Me Dad wouldn't let me go to sea. After a bit I ended up

The Storr fishermen today. *From left to right*: Richard, Matty and George

going into the Merchant Navy. Then Georgie Storr got me a job. Straightaway I went fishing, and me Dad couldn't say nowt, 'cos I wasn't living with him.'

The group all nodded with vigorous understanding. Chris Hall emphasised the strength of feeling in family continuity: 'When I was at school I was keen on farming, fishing was nowt to me. But my brothers, William, John, and Eric, were all fishermen, and so was my father, my uncle and lots more relations. It went back for generations. So eventually I went under my brother William. I was with him two months. We were potting, then we had a fight and he just kicked me out. That's how fishing is. Never mind family, if you argue with the skipper, he's the boss and you're out. Mind you, my father told me not to go fishing. But with me my life was fishing boats, see.'

With quiet pride one of them said: 'When you go back in our family, especially on the lads' side, the first thing all of them wanted to do was go through their father's footsteps.' This group, pouring down pints faster than was good for them because it was the weekend, was none the less impressive. Where else could you find a bunch of teenagers talking so openly and deliberately about being proud to follow in their father's footsteps?

Looking back now, Georgie Storr sees it from a father's point of view: 'That boy of mine, Colin, he says he's going, but if he has my wish, I would say no. But there you are, if he wants to go why should I stop him? If your father's fishing and you get aboard the boats when you're still at school, you keep saying to yourself, "When I leave school, I'm going to be a fisherman!"'

Dockland, Hull

'My Dad died at 62. He'd worked hard all his life on the dock, and at the end of the day what had my mother got? A few sticks of furniture and a hundred pound from the National Dock Labour Board. It made me look at politics a bit closer . . .'

To most natives of Hull the docks are a world apart. They are isolated from the city centre, and east of the River Hull which runs north to south into the Humber. The tall cranes are scarcely visible in West Hull, except from the tower blocks of the housing estates that have sprung up since the Second World War, although the functional sheds and acres of grey water stretch for miles along the bleak north bank of the Humber.

But it is not the high fences along Hedon Road that make the docks an alien world to the vast majority of Hull's three hundred thousand citizens, so much as the character, customs and work experience of the dockers themselves, now reduced to a work-force of under two thousand. In a city where ten per cent of the workforce is unemployed, and where the once huge and valuable fishing industry has all but closed down, Hull's dockers are not exactly popular, since they have the reputation of being among the most militant in the country. Even their generosity in a good cause does not receive quite the publicity it might seem to deserve.

Walter Cunningham, still among the most vigorous of shop stewards' leaders in the port, illustrated the rift between town and dockers with a recent story: 'After our last pay talks we had quite a large amount of back pay to be drawn. There'd been an appeal by some of the surgeons at the General Hospital for a laser gun which was going to cost £20,000, so at the mass meeting a docker – just an ordinary docker – stood up and suggested that every docker should give ten pounds of his back pay to the laser fund. And, of course, it was carried unanimously, the money was stopped out of our pay, and the £20,000 went straight to the surgeons. Well, that rated about a two-inch piece in the local paper. Whereas if we'd been coming

Hull docks: engraving of 1829

out on a day's token strike, we'd have rated banner headlines!'

The gap between town and dockland seems to be a relic of their differing origins and separate communities. Most of the dockers' families arrived in East Hull some time after 1850, when the great expansion of the commercial docks began. There were Cornish and Irish immigrants who came to dig the docks and stayed to work them, but most were the impoverished rural families who migrated from all parts, especially northern England and the Borders, to any of the nineteenth-century sites of industrial expansion on the promise of a brighter future. Once settled around the docks, these migrants in an alien land turned inwards, held together by one common bond – their work. That remained true for almost a hundred years – until after the Second World War when a massive programme of slum clearance, together with easier transport, made dispersal inevitable.

In this self-protective but vulnerable society, the seeds of conflict were sown early, long before 'organised labour' was a force to con-

Aerial view today. Alexandra Docks in centre, King George and Queen
Elizabeth Docks beyond

sider. In 1893 for example, miners from Lancashire and Yorkshire
were brought in to break a dock strike, and made themselves doubly
unpopular by clinking the money in their pockets. To this day, some
Hull dockers do not speak kindly of miners. Memories in such self-
contained areas of industrial relations are long, though on occasion
illogical – one could no more imagine Yorkshire miners strike-
breaking today than dockers voting contributions to the Confeder-
ation of British Industry.

In spite of the relatively recent origins of Hull's docking community, the port to which this workforce came has been established
far longer than a century. Before 1300 Hull was, in terms of custom
value, the third port in the land, after only London and Boston, and
right down to the mid-eighteenth century its life was governed by
the merchants whose ships crowded the wharves and quays along the
River Hull. So successful was the trade by this period that in 1774 the
City Fathers promoted an Act of Parliament to build the first dock, 'a

bason for light ships', whose public wharves would incidentally make it easier to collect customs dues and suppress smuggling.

During the next hundred years the whole chain of Town Docks was built and Hull's trade flourished, but despite its prosperity the city remained largely isolated from the rest of the country. Part of that isolation was simply geographical. Until well into the nineteenth century the trip to Rotterdam was quicker than that to London, and if the rest of Yorkshire has in this century seen Hull as 'a gateway to Europe', Hull has always felt close links with the Continent, long before anyone mentioned the EEC. Those long-term connections with Holland and Scandinavia are still evident in the architecture of the Old Town, a few street names, and road signs in four languages.

In its relations with the rest of England, Hull has long practised self-reliance, but in some ways the city seems unable to decide whether it is a village or an international city. As writer Alan Plater, who has lived in Hull since he was three, describes it: 'Hull is a big city but it still retains something of the intimate small-town atmosphere that means if you say Hello to a man, he doesn't immediately wonder what your angle is!'

For all their natural friendliness, Plater argues that the people of Hull suffer from an unjustified lack of self-confidence: 'If we get things right, we tend to be apologetic, and too much of the time we're content to be runners–up, fastest losers, gallant in defeat . . . the two Rugby League teams, full of smashing players, have never managed to *win* a Cup Final at Wembley . . .'

Obviously he was speaking before May 1980 when the two teams, Hull Kingston Rovers and just plain Hull, played each other in the Challenge Cup Final at Wembley. Ron Turner, Secretary of Hull Kingston Rovers, when asked beforehand why he was none too pleased about such a match, said pointedly: 'Because one of us has to lose'. Although Rovers brought home the cup, it would have felt better by far to snatch it away from some other town's team. Traditionally, Hull Kingston Rovers, based at Craven Park in East Hull, had been the dockers' team, while the fishermen of West Hull supported the rival Hull team. As a parallel work tradition that had grown up in West Hull after the start of trawling in the 1840s, the fishermen were considered worthy rivals. Now, with the sad collapse of the fishing fleet in the last few years, the Hull team has less and less

Foremen choosing their workers in the Pen, 1967

connection with fishing, though Rovers still fields a team including four or five sons of dockers.

The dockers' workforce too has declined dramatically in the last twelve years, though this has been due more to such factors as containerisation rather than to any loss of trade. Recruitment has been almost non-existent, and consequently while numbers have fallen from four thousand one hundred and fifty-three in 1967 to about one thousand nine hundred in 1980, the average age of the Hull docker has risen to forty-seven. So perhaps it is not surprising to find that the character of the dockers is dominated by their memory of the old days – a far from romantic past. Even dockers of no more than thirty-five remember the days of the 'Pen', the system by which most men were hired before 1967. It was casual employment, the foreman picking his own gang for each ship from the dockers massed before him. Everyone now agrees that it was degrading, but this was the system that operated for most of the men until September 1967, after the Devlin Report had recommended the total de-casualisation of dock work. Even now each Monday morning hundreds of men pack into the 'Control', a bleak brick and concrete hall, to hear their work allocated by loudspeaker. The atmosphere has been calmed by a guaranteed minimum wage, but otherwise it is not far removed from scenes of the 'Pen' in an old publicity film made unselfconsciously by one of the port's shippers in 1948 to promote their business.

In the worst days, dockers climbed on each other's backs in the 'Pen' for survival, though outside the gates they had developed a society that was fiercely and communally self-protective. That atmosphere still persists, and must in part be held responsible for the continuing divide between dockers and city, but it also provides a springboard for welfare activities among their own old folk. Much of the funds these days, as well as a Welfare Officer, come from the National Dock Labour Board, paid for by an employers' levy, but the Gangwayenders' and Evergreens' Clubs are organised by retired dock workers for themselves and their wives. They use the dockers' own club, The Willows, in Holderness Road. Here the old folk meet on Tuesday and Wednesday afternoons to have a drink, a game of bingo or snooker and, inevitably, to swap yarns about the old days. Highlights of the year are coach trips to, of all places, other people's docks!

In November 1979, on a Tuesday when The Willows Club was needed during the day to set out the dockers' annual Chrysanthemum Show, four coaches set out from Hull taking the Evergreens on a visit to the smaller port of Goole, thirty miles up the Humber. In the dockers' club the Goole Good Companions had laid on a splendid welcome – hot pies, sandwiches and home-made cakes, bingo, dancing and a lady accordionist with a vast repertoire of old favourites like 'Strollin' and 'Roll out the Barrel'.

Most of the visitors stayed inside the club for the bingo, but, fortified with a couple of drinks, half a dozen of the Hull lads and a few of Goole's retired dockers did brave the cold for a quick look at the sights of Goole docks. There were technical questions about types of ropes and lifting capacities of cranes, and when innovations in the modernised Goole docks proved too much for the retired Goole men, the conversation drifted into an exchange of old tales. It was dark by the time they all piled back on the coach for a sing-song on the way home. Those who still had the energy went back into the Willows Club for the Chrysanthemum Show, to proclaim the old boast that 'nobody grows chrysanthemums like a docker'.

Treasurer of the Evergreens, and just about everything else from coach tour guide to bingo caller, is seventy-three-year-old Alfie Hudson, whose energy makes you almost miss the joke when he talks about the difficulties of organising 'these old folks'. Alfie worked on the docks all his life, but now his chief passion is gardening, where his organising abilities have also brought him office. Though he has offered to hand the job over to anyone who will show an interest, for the present he is secretary of the Mayberry Allotment Association, where plots are laid out in numbered ranks like sheds on the docks. Alfie's own plot is on a smaller piece of land away from the main block of two hundred allotments, which are boxed in by council houses. This, he says, is to avoid being constantly pestered by other allotment holders seeking advice and information. His plot has an additional attraction – it is next door to a large pub which he calls 'The Red 'Ell'. 'The Blue 'Eaven' is just up the road. These pubs are in fact called 'The Crown' and 'The Anchor' but, like most foremen on the docks, they have nicknames, apparently relating to the colour of their floodlighting.

Each morning Alfie cycles the few hundred yards from his home to the allotment shop to check it is open for business, before going on to his own allotment to put in 'an hour or so'. Then, soon after twelve, he makes for 'The Red 'Ell', before going home for his midday meal. Such is the regularity of his visits to the pub that one story has it he keeps his tools there, though he expressed amazement that his wife could tell us where to look for him. Even after years in retirement he seems to maintain the rhythm of his working life on the docks. When Alfie started it was anything but a secure job: 'Any Tom, Dick or Harry could go on the dock. A foreman could tell me, or anyone he liked, he had a ship coming in. If your face fitted, you got taken on. A lot of men had jobs in the winter, and when that slackened off, they used to come on the dock for the summer, like coalmen for instance, because there wasn't so much demand for coal in the summer. We were gangway enders when I started in the early 1930s – that's where we got the name of the club from. You just went to a ship and stood at the end of the gangways to the holds. You knew by the ship and its cargo how many gangs they'd need and which holds were best. With the "Pen" system you could take your chance a bit, but they usually left the good ships while they manned up the bad ones. But imagine one hundred and fifty or two hundred men in there and a wool ship

Unloading timber *c.* 1925

came in. By the time you got your book up and waved it at the foreman, you'd be pinned up against the wall – "the wailing wall" we called it. I've had fellows climbing on my back for jobs on a wool ship.'

In those days every docker had to own and carry a bag of murderous-looking tools. In slacker periods, getting a job after a spell without work, would mean redeeming tools from the pawn shop. And, as Alfie recalls, even then life could be tough: 'I've broken my tommy hook on pit-props thick with ice. With a cargo of dirty barley you wanted a nylon stocking over your face for a mask and another pair of your wife's stockings over your boots. Otherwise you'd come home with the spikes of barley chafing your legs. Still, you could empty your shoes and give it to the chickens! With beef you could have a two hundred and forty-pound load to lift, but butter and canned stuff were the good jobs because of the bonuses.'

This is the world that bred local activists like Walter Cunningham.

He was born in the old Drypool area of dockland where the River Hull flows into the Humber. The Victoria Dock where his father humped timber has been filled in and most of the cramped terraces have gone, but Walter has not forgotten the picture: 'The thing that has changed dramatically is the noise, the squeal of saws working at Smith's, the big timber yard, and sawdust constantly all over the street. Those places were built simply because of the timber imported into the Victoria Dock. As kids we either played in the streets or went on to the docks, playing in the timber pond, making rafts, until we were chased out by the police for one thing or another. In fact our playground was the docks. We used to watch the dockers playing "Crown and An-chor" and look out for the police for them. It was a lot rougher then than it is now. I've seen my dad in plenty of fights when he came home from the pub. They were rough, hard men in those days.

'My dad ran timber, really hard work, and he died, basically I thought through hard work, at sixty-two. It made me start thinking – my dad's died at sixty-two, worked hard all his life on the dock, and at the end of the day what's my mother got? A few sticks of furniture and a hundred pounds from the National Dock Labour Board. It made me look at politics a bit closer, although even today I'm not really a political animal. Now I just want to get the best possible deal from the employers for the dockers.'

Arriving at that 'deal' has not always been straightforward for Walter and men of like mind, nor has it been easy for those who have sat across the table from them. Walter is still very active on the Shop Stewards' Committee which is referred to by the employers as 'unofficial', but he is quite clear about why the shop stewards by-passed the Transport and General Workers' Union which officially represents most of the dockers, in favour of their own on-the-spot, work-place action: 'We set up an unofficial committee which was divorced completely from the Union because we thought the Union wasn't doing enough. You begin to realise that the only way to get the Union to work is for you to make it work.'

The emphasis was once again on the self-help and self-protection so evident in the retired dockers' clubs. But we suggested that this kind of 'militant' behaviour might be seen in another light, and put to him the famous question of the McCarthy Trials, was he, or had he ever been, a member of the Communist Party? 'People like myself, who stand out on occasion, tend to get labels put on them, but I've never belonged to the Communist Party, never really wanted to, nor any other extreme left wing party. I do belong to the Labour Party, but I don't get involved as much as I would like because of the work I do on the docks.'

Occasionally Walter's determination to get what he now sees as the dockers' rights has erupted into clashes with authority. In 1972 he hit the national headlines for his prominent part in the Hull dockers' campaign against the use of unregistered ports. The campaign included the notorious Neap House Wharf confrontation, when hundreds of Hull dockers, picketing one small port on the south side of the Humber, clashed violently with the police. However the scale of trouble was small compared with the strike of 1893 when there were Admiralty gun-boats in the Humber, timber stores were set on fire, and all available firearms were bought up from Hull's gunsmiths.

Walter explained their case: 'The Devlin Report gave us the best deal as dockworkers that we'd ever had. It meant everybody was with a permanent employer and had a guaranteed wage. But after that the work started to leave the registered ports and began to seep into the unregistered ports where the men were not unionised and the rates and conditions were very poor. The smaller traffic which we took on the Western docks at Hull was being completely lost to the unregistered wharves. We did succeed in getting most of the small ports closed, but somebody somewhere had made the decision that Neap House Wharf was going to stay open. That's how we came into conflict with the police there. But we still haven't solved the problem. They're still expanding the unregistered wharves and quays.'

Though many have disagreed with his actions, there can be little doubt about the sincerity of Walter's commitment. Going out on a limb in this way has cost him a lot. In an introverted city like Hull, local affairs, particularly as they are affected by the docks, assume sizeable proportions, and some people have not been slow to show their feelings: 'I've had a few anonymous letters and the telephone, of course, had to go ex-directory. I think the kids could have been affected to a certain extent at school. But I've got a great family and even the kids used to support me in what I was doing. My wife sees eye to eye with me, so I've never had to live with conflict at home. I'd never have been able to carry on for twelve years without the support I got from my home.'

As might be expected, two of Walter's sons have put their names down on the docker's waiting list, and the third has had the formal training in industrial studies that Walter never had. Even his daughter Rosemary added her name to the list as soon as the Equal Opportunities Bill became law. The list itself is more exclusive than that for Eton College. Only sons (and now daughters!) of dockers are eligible for enrolment at sixteen and their names are automatically struck off when they reach the age of thirty-two. There were no recruitments from the list at all from 1967 to 1975, apart from twelve lightermen in 1971, and since 1975 the less than fifty a year recruited have all been specialists, such as tally-clerks and fork-lift truck drivers. The attractions of dock work to the young today are obviously security, relatively good pay for short hours, an outdoor life and, because they are all docker's sons, familiarity with the tradition. But very few of the one thousand and sixty-seven on the list in early 1980 are likely to experience life on the docks today at first hand.

The 'Control', where the dockers report shortly before 8 am for the allocation of work, serves basically the same purpose as the old 'Pen'. It is still strictly functional, but the days of the all-powerful foreman and the waving of books have gone. Over the loudspeaker the men are assigned to ships by an official of Hull and Humber Cargo Handling Ltd., which now employs the vast majority of dockers and is a wholly-owned subsidiary of the British Transport Docks Board. Work is allocated very strictly on a rota system, and once their names are called out, the men hand in their books at one of a row of windows, any absentees being replaced by those next on the list. Any still without work will then 'dint', that is have their books stamped for the guaranteed minimum wage, about £2 less than a standard day's pay, until the arrival of more ships in port brings their turn round again. A few who know they are at the bottom of the list will turn up with a garden fork already strapped to their bike or with decorators' ladders on the roof-rack. The working majority make off to their ships on bikes and mopeds, or in cars. Though most jobs these days are mechanised, some of them can still be dirty or unpleasant, such as unloading bauxite powder, working in refrigerated holds, or discharging the stinking shea nuts that go upriver in barges for the manufacture of margarine. The skills are more obvious during loading, when it can be quite amazing to watch men on fork-lift trucks deftly pack many tons of machinery into the tight corners of awkward holds. Such efficient use of space may well find the foremen being

Loading steel in 1980 on King George Dock

entertained in the Chief Officers' cabin to cans of lager at the end of
the afternoon.

Apart from such perks there is little now to distinguish foremen
from dockers, a distinct absence of any 'master and man' atmosphere.
Foremen are dockers who have been promoted, but that no longer
makes them 'bosses' men', though the wisecracks still fly in both
directions. The dockers have nicknames for all the foremen, such
as Skippy, Tween-decks Ghost, Bungalow ('nothing upstairs') and
Rembrandt ('Gather round lads, and I'll put you in the picture'). The
foremen in reply suggest that 'Vermeer should have come to Hull
Docks to paint his still-life'. The sense of humour is most often wry
and gentle, rather than vicious, with graffiti such as 'Walter Cunny
walks on water, Tra-la-la la la!' leavening the usual mix of 'Thatcher
Out!' and 'Commies, go to Russia!' More passions are aroused when
the conversations, or the graffiti, turn to Rugby League, as millions of

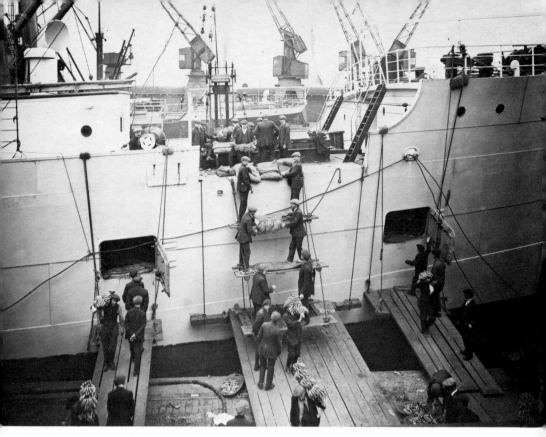

Discharging a cargo of bananas on King George Dock *c.* 1930

television viewers saw when most of Hull's dockers cheered their team to victory at Wembley.

Two of the proudest fathers in dockland are Peter Smith, a shed foreman, whose son Mike is an international centre, and Bernard Rose, a deckman, whose son Paul has played forward for Great Britain. Both sons play for Hull Kingston Rovers, and naturally both have their names down on the dockers' list. Bernard, who has been on the docks for thirty years, described the attractions of the job today compared with when he began: 'In the old days everything was piece work. Today we don't seem to rush about like we did twenty years ago. People were getting killed or seriously injured then through trying to get out as much tonnage as possible to earn more money.'

Both Bernard and Peter agreed that shop stewards like Walter Cunningham played a big part in making the job safer and better. Bernard in particular had no doubts: 'I think the shop stewards can

Bernard Rose at the controls of a deck crane

take a lot of credit for the changes, but you see we stick together. If there was a strike, it wouldn't be half against half. It's everybody's living on the docks, and if we had to, ninety per cent of us would come out on strike. It's always been for a good cause in the end.'

As well as 'worker solidarity', the pull of family tradition came out strongly too, especially in Bernard's case: 'I'd like to see Paul come on the docks. All the family's been on the docks for generations but it's up to him when the time comes.'

Whether that time will ever come seems unlikely at the present rate of recruitment for either Paul or Mike, though both of them admit the hours and the system of voluntary overtime would leave plenty of time for their rugby. Paul Rose is twenty-eight and works as a fitter for a ship repair firm, and Mike Smith is twenty-two. He is working for BP as an electrician's mate while looking for a good opening in his original trade as a joiner, but he has his doubts now about the docks: 'It doesn't seem so secure as it was, say, five or six years ago. I put my name down because it was a secure job, it was a busy port. But now the fish docks have closed down, and I think it's all dying out slowly.'

The use of containers has obviously been a major factor in reducing the need for a large workforce, but we asked Walter Cunningham whether he and his campaigning colleagues would accept responsibility for any run-down there might have been in Hull Docks. His first thought was to wonder whether they had made a mistake in not pursuing to the death their campaign against unregistered ports, particularly since the issue still remained to be resolved: 'I think we've got to decide in the near future whether we're going to be in conflict with them again or whether we're going to compete with them. To be quite honest, I think we're all getting too bloody old to be going down there and start picketing again.'

The dockers' average age of forty-seven is on everyone's mind. Walter stressed the need for new blood but realised the dilemma of trying to achieve this against the background of a reducing labour force. He pointed to a period of five or six years free from major disputes, but conceded that the port was still relatively expensive, although Hull men, he emphasised, had a widespread reputation for being good at handling all sorts of cargoes and stowing vessels, 'so where we're a bit more expensive than other ports, we can make up for that by getting more cubic capacity into vessels'.

For those on his side of the negotiating fence he sees the grey face of bureaucracy as the greatest problem today: 'Before I was on the negotiating committee, we were just dealing with people, the employers, who had a licence to print money. The only motivation was profit, nothing else. They didn't want to put anything back into the port and I don't think they ever did. When Devlin came in, it meant we had a lot fewer employers to deal with, and I think their attitude did change considerably. But now it's changed again with the British Transport Docks Board getting involved, and everything has to be funnelled through Melbury House in London, which to my way of thinking is totally wrong. If I have to negotiate with people, I want to be sitting with them, not with people who are only being told what to do from somewhere else.'

Ironically for these Hull men, who by-passed their own Union in favour of local control of local issues, the other side of the table now seems to have moved away from local control. Many of the British Transport Docks Board representatives who sit opposite the dockers in the monthly Port Joint Working Committee meetings are Hull men, but the ultimate control lies in London.

One of these men is Geoffrey Cullington, the Docks' Manager, who still lives on one of the broad avenues of pre-war semis that characterise the suburbs of Hull. He was formerly Managing Director of Hull and Humber Cargo Handling Ltd, the stevedoring company which still employs four-fifths of Hull's dockers, and is now run by his cousin Denis Cullington for the Docks Board. The firm was started in 1913 by Geoffrey's father who was soon joined by his brother, Denis's father. When they came out of the forces after the last war, the cousins joined their fathers in the business. Geoffrey Cullington is quietly-spoken, unpretentious and as proud of his Hull origins as the dockers, but as one might expect, he saw the old days of the 'Pen' in a quite different light from 'the workpeople': 'As an employer, I did not consider that it was an injustice at all. After the war we had a system in Hull of "weekly workers", whereby each firm chose for itself a number of men and borrowed from the Dock Labour Board to make up the numbers. It suited us because we got some good men, and I think you could say that basically the work-shy were left on the bench. It suited the employers but it certainly didn't suit the men. They called it the "blue-eye" system – the bosses' blue-eyed boys got all the best jobs. But it was simply that some people worked better and faster than others, and they were the ones who were taken first. Some of the others were so sure of being unemployed that they even ran taxi businesses!'

To the employers, the Devlin Report, with its insistence that every dock worker must have a permanent employer, was not the god-send it seemed to the workers: 'We didn't like it at all, because everybody volunteered to go to those firms which had the most lucrative business. And we all had to take, I think, twenty-five per cent more than our requirements because of the labour surplus. Piecework was the system then, and I still think it's a very good thing. You get a good out-turn, but if everything isn't absolutely normal the cry goes up, "This is affecting our piecework, we've got to have some more money." So we had all sorts of troubles.'

Rather like Walter Cunningham, Geoffrey Cullington now has the air of a philosophical veteran of the struggle: 'When I became Chairman of the Port Employers, I made it my business to achieve some sort of rapport with the shop stewards, and I think events proved that I did that. What we need here now are two things, a reliable record of industrial peace and the ability to do the job at a competitive price.

Left: Geoffrey Cullington, docks manager for the British Transport Docks Board; *right*: Walter Cunningham, one of the leaders of the 'unofficial' shop stewards' committee

The shop stewards will tell you that, as far as I am concerned, I want to put them all in a container and dump it in the middle of the North Sea! On the whole, though, they had shown themselves pretty responsible until the awful winter of 1978. Then a long series of one-day strikes gave us a lot of problems. We'd had almost five years of peace until then – when there was a problem, they got in touch with me and we sat round a table and ironed it out.'

Geoffrey Cullington's emphasis on local people dealing with local problems is supported by Walter Cunningham. Both are Hull men born and bred, and this seems to have produced a measure of understanding. As Walter says: 'We don't see a great deal of the employers socially, but we get on quite well with them. You've got to remember that some of the employers had fathers who were dockers, and some of their families were in the industry. So we've all got the same background knowledge of the docks, you see.'

Sidney Sussex College, Cambridge

'There is much to be said for an intimate community with a strong corporate spirit . . .' (C. W. Scott-Giles Sidney Sussex College, a Short History, *1950)*

On a bright Saturday afternoon in February, one of Cambridge University's oldest and most colourful rituals was reaching its climax – it was the last day of the Lent Races, universally called by both town and gown 'The Bumps'. The River Cam, known derisively in Oxford as 'the Ditch', is too narrow even for two eights to row side by side, so the objective of the single-file races is to bump the boat in front. The towpath from First Post Corner to the 'Pike and Eel' was packed with excited students and ex-students of all ages, cheering the straining crews.

Each boat was accompanied by a posse of cyclists, among them the coach with a loud-hailer, urging on their champions. The cyclists had scant regard for anyone in their path, or for themselves, as one spectacular pile-up amply demonstrated. Outside the 'Plough' at Fen Ditton a beery throng, crammed on to a wooden jetty marked 'Danger – Keep Off' sang and jeered. At least one of their number would end up in the Cam before the First Division boats went past at quarter to five. Harry Littlechild surveyed the familiar scene with the air of an old hand.

Harry first came to the towpath in 1924 when he began his rowing career with the College Servants' Club. In 1974 he retired after fifty years of service to Sidney Sussex College, where since the Second World War he had been Catering Manager. His particular interest was to check the progress of the Sidney Sussex second boat. For eight years, from 1946, he had been its coach, an unheard of position before the war for a college servant, as he recalls: 'After the war there were very few young people coming up to University who had much

The Lent Bumps, 1980

knowledge of rowing. The boat captain, through various means, got to know that I'd done a bit of rowing and he asked me if I would coach a boat. I said yes, I'd love to, and in one spell I took the Sidney second boat up eleven places in two years. They've asked me to go back this year and dabble with them again, but I don't know – I'll have to see.'

So Harry's interest in the Bumps was far from academic, and his excitement was real enough when, just on Grassy Corner in front of him, a lady cox, an innovation since Harry's day, coaxed the Sidney second boat to their third bump in four days.

Sidney Sussex is not the most fashionable of Cambridge colleges. Though formally constituted in 1596 by provision made in the will of Lady Frances Sidney, Countess of Sussex, it lacks the architectural grandeur of King's, or the social cachet of Trinity or Magdalene. But as C. W. Scott-Giles writes in his *Short History* of the College:

Sidney Sussex College, Cambridge 109

Sidney Sussex College, founded 1596

There is something to be said for a place which retains the academic privacy and quietude which the renowned beauty spots are apt to lose. Under the creeper-clad tower, the gates stand open to a busy street, but few visitors give more than a glance into the courts. Those who penetrate the unimposing façade are rewarded by the discovery of the most beautiful modern chapel in the University, an old garden of great loveliness, and evidence of an historic past in portraits in the Hall. Well may one wonder why a writer on Cambridge has dismissed this College in the words, *Passing by Sidney, which has nothing to detain us . . .*

The college as an institution has attractions which run deeper than the appearance of its buildings. With just over three hundred under-graduates, seventy graduates and forty-two Fellows, and around ninety staff including part-timers, Sidney Sussex, most of them feel, is just about the right size for everyone to know everyone else. Many of the larger colleges have now abandoned traditional staffing arrangements and turned to business methods and catering companies, and relationships have inevitably become more impersonal, but Sidney Sussex retains a family feeling that includes the staff, no longer officially referred to as 'college servants'. Sons and daughters still follow on into college service as they doubtless did when Oliver Cromwell was a Fellow commoner. And though some of the long-serving lady bedmakers may question the propriety of male and female undergraduates living in on mixed staircases, they can still bask in the reflected glory of a college that has twice won ITV's *University Challenge*!

It was no surprise that when Harry Littlechild began writing his memoirs of fifty years' service to the college, the first to offer advice and assistance was the distinguished medieval historian, Dr R. C. Smail, a fellow of the college and keeper of its archives. He seemed intrigued at the prospect of college history seen from a new angle, and set out to encourage Harry's remarkable memory for detail: 'I spent a lot of my young life at King's, and then I was a choirboy at Trinity, so everyone thought I would go to one or the other. But then a friend of mine who was an apprentice at St Catherine's painted such a wonderful picture of work in the kitchen that I went straight home to my father and said, "Dad, I want to be a chef". He knew several people at Sidney and, within four days of my wanting to be a chef, I was accepted as an apprentice there at five shillings a week. During the long vacations they used to sack some of the junior cooks and kitchen porters, but allowed the apprentice boys to go on seasonal jobs. I remember when I was eighteen going on a seasonal job to Scotland. My college pay was then ten shillings a week, and they offered me three pound fifteen shillings a week living in. My father just couldn't believe it.'

The job to which Harry was apprenticed in college involved much more than the preparation of food. He was catering to the personal tastes of young gentlemen, usually well-off, who lived both in and out of college: 'In the 1920s and 30s we sent dinner parties out all over Cambridge, six course meals sent by relays of kitchen porters with trays on their heads. You'd see them anywhere in town between seven and nine o'clock at night. All the stuff was put into silver entrée dishes which held the heat, and then we used to wrap the trays in green baize. I never remember anyone having a cold meal arrive at the house. In fact, we used to send one chap his breakfast nearly half a mile every

Harry Littlechild: behind him, the Founder's portrait

A bevy of bedmakers – Joyce Waterfall is centre front, and her sister Louise Langford, front right

day because his landlady wouldn't cook him breakfast. Another thing we liked about the undergraduates then was that if they did any damage anywhere, they clubbed together, the cheque was signed and off it went.'

Though the life-style of undergraduates may have changed in many respects, quite a large proportion of them, as well as the unmarried Fellows, still live in rooms on the staircases around the college courts. There they are tidied up daily by the bedmakers, one thriving example at least of Cambridge domestic traditions. From about 7 am, when few students are abroad, droves of ladies, on foot or the universal bicycle with front basket, can be seen hurrying to the colleges and their particular staircase. In Sidney Sussex College, long service is still the norm and the mother-to-daughter tradition still in evidence. Vera Taylor, with eighteen years' service, was brought in by her mother who put in fifty years before she retired. Joyce Waterfall who has been at the college for thirty years, twenty-two of them on x staircase, recently brought in her sister, Louise Langford. She took on the Combination Room (Senior Common Room) and Fellows' Parlour rather than a staircase because she 'couldn't face cleaning lavatories!' Their sister-in-law Mrs Franklin, who cleans the library and surgery, has been there for twenty years, and their brother Keith comes in as a waiter on special occasions too.

The biggest changes in college life came with the war, but ladies with long service since then, like Mrs Waterfall, have found quite a few innovations. Perhaps the biggest shock to the system was the recent introduction of 'young ladies' amongst the 'young gentlemen', but the bedmakers are a long-suffering and even-tempered race, and Mrs Waterfall soon adjusted: 'This was the first year I'd had girls. I didn't want to look after girls, to be honest with you. I thought they'd be a nuisance with washing about and so on, but I was wrong, they're really smashing.'

Some adjustments though have been harder to make and a slackening of the rules governing the 'young gentlemen' has not always made for an easy life: 'When I first came here the boys never had girls in their rooms like they do now. Now they're allowed to have any of their friends sleep in their rooms for three nights. Last year I had four boys and it was a terrible year. I didn't know whether to pack it in or not, they were really terrible, drink problems, girls, you know. Some years you just can't talk to them, you just go into their room and get out as quick as you can. And then you get a good batch, and they're really fun to be with.'

Vera Taylor, warm-hearted and talkative, like a Cambridge Gracie Fields, liked the atmosphere and would never dream of trying another college: 'I wouldn't want to try another college after this one. Everybody's so friendly here, it's like a family. There's no distinction between anybody. But having children of your own makes a lot of difference. I live on my own now, so I like the company.' Vera gets on well with the girls, but she still looks back on the old men-only days as the best: 'We had more fun with the boys than we do with the girls. I think if you treat them like your own boys, you do get on with them, but I don't think you get the fun quite the same with the girls. Maybe it's with me not having had daughters – you don't have to handle them quite the same as boys, do you?'

Though the first woman Fellow was admitted to the college in

1975, there have undoubtedly been more changes in the world of the undergraduates than that of the Fellows, where a strong undercurrent of ritual persists. One such observance is the taking of wine in the Combination Room each Friday night during term-time. Denis Pettit, the long-serving Fellows' Waiter, prepares the panelled room for them by arranging the richly-polished rosewood tables in their interlocking arc, setting out an exact number of chairs and place-settings in silver, placing the decanters on the tables and finally lighting the candles. He then withdraws to signal discreetly to the Master on high table in the Hall that all is ready. The Master then leads the senior members of college into the Combination Room to take wine, dessert and coffee, an occasion which also serves the useful purpose of allowing the Fellows to discuss quite privately and informally matters of current interest in the college.

Even though Sidney Sussex has a long-standing reputation among college staff in Cambridge for close relations between its academics and the 'servants', the gap has narrowed more rapidly in recent years. In Harry Littlechild's time certain of his better acquaintances among the academics came to call him 'Harry', but for the most part to him they were still 'Sir'. Now when Michael Daynes, the second chef, draws up the match list for the end-of-term darts matches involving both staff and Fellows, the only noticeable distinction is Christian names for the staff and 'Dr' or 'Mr' for the Fellows.

These matches take place in the suitably modern surroundings of the Junior Common Room in Blundell Court, a new block stretching back into the gardens behind the college. Significantly Fellows and staff play not against each other, but in 'mixed' doubles. Little else is of significance, since no one seemed to care who won, and once the convivial atmosphere of the evening was under way, there was little to distinguish staff from academics. Certainly some of the kitchen staff showed skills practised in hostelries elsewhere, but in the thick of it too, chalking up quite respectable scores, were Roger Andrew, the Bursar, the Dean, Paul Dawson, and, in civvies, the chaplain, Michael Wadsworth.

Harry Littlechild, back in college for the evening, took on Ernie Green, still the Master's Butler. Between them they have put in ninety-eight years at the college. Some of the older hands, like Ernie, who came to Sidney Sussex in 1932, are still a little bemused by the informality of such gatherings, but Ernie is in no doubt about the rewards the family atmosphere has given him over his forty-eight years. He said warmly: 'It's a beautiful life, is college life. Being always with young people keeps you young.'

Ernie came to the college at the wish of his father who, like his father before him, did maintenance work on the college and its lodging houses. His recollections show some tinge of regret for the passing of more formal days: 'We used to have a dark suit, black tie and bowler hat in the old days. When I served on the top table I wore tails, frock-coat and butterfly bow. But all that fell through.'

Apart from the security that such a job offered in the early thirties, there were occasional flashes of generosity by the college authorities which Ernie remembers with touching appreciation: 'They asked me to take notes round the colleges and labs, and after a while Major Temple bought a bicycle for me. After I'd had it a year, he called me up to his rooms and said I had to pay half the cost, but after another six months he called me up again and said it was mine. I wasn't allowed to take it home before it was mine, but I had that Raleigh for years afterwards. It was a lovely bike. It only cost £5/19/6, the bell and the bag on the back were extra, but it was very, very nice.'

As Harry Littlechild remembers, Sidney's Bursar was friendly enough, even in those days, to come down and talk to him in the kitchen, but for the most part college servants walked in fear of the wrath of Deans and Bursars, and Harry was no exception: 'When we were young lads in the kitchen, we used to kick around paper balls done up with rubber bands in South Court, which was a staff court. One day Ike Green, Ernie Green's father, reported all the drains were blocked with these balls, so Major Davenport, who was then the Bursar, said anybody found kicking these missiles about would be immediately dismissed from the college. Well, I was going through the court and I saw one of these things, took a kick at it and it went straight through a window. I went running round to the glazier who was putting some windows in Garden Court, and hauled him round to replace the glass. He did it straightaway, and Mrs Taylor the bed-maker cleaned the mess up. I rubbed some dirt round the putty so it didn't look so new, and I never heard any more about it.'

Somehow one does not gain the impression that Brian Barber, who took over the kitchens when Harry retired, or his colleague Bob Page, the steward's clerk who pays out staff wages, go in such fear and trembling of their employers. Both are highly respectful of tradition,

College staff: *front row, left to right*, Bob Page, Brian Barber, the Bursar,
Denis Pettit, Albert Flack; *centre, middle row*, Ernie Green

but modern-minded in their work methods and decidedly unim-
pressed by any continuing references to 'college servants'. Coinciden-
tally both of them spent several years at Churchill College, a post-war
foundation with correspondingly young traditions.

   Bob Page though, whose mother is a bedmaker in one of the college
hostels, served an almost traditional old-style apprenticeship to college life: 'I first came here nineteen years ago as a part-time waiter
when I was sixteen and still at the Tech. Two years later I took a full-
time job in the office at Churchill, but I kept the waiting going at
Sidney for nine years altogether. I came here full-time five and a half
years ago now. You got a lot of public school types in my early days.
I remember one of them saying to me after he'd been here about a
week, "You should call me 'sir'." So I said to him, "Why, you been

knighted or something!" It didn't go down too well, but over his three years here he turned out to be one of the nicest blokes to get along with. I think there's a more friendly atmosphere now, because most of the students who are here are from the same background as myself – a working-class background. Mind you, I reckon the pranks were a lot better performed in the old days.'

Even so, he had to admit that, from the evidence of his own photographs, rowing club stunts in the past couple of years had not been bad. Not long ago the college woke one morning to find estate agents' boards reading *College for Sale* strung up along the front wall, and on another occasion to discover that a recently laid-out rockery had been transformed overnight into a fish-pond, complete with plastic ducks. Bob related some of the changes to the way students are financed these days, which he sees as he hands out the maintenance grants at the beginning of each term: 'I'd say that ninety-five per cent of the students receive a grant now, as compared with about seventy per cent when I began. The self-sponsored ones were possibly those that we had most trouble with getting our money back. I think a lot of them had to wait for the right horse to come in before they paid their bills!'

Although he was subject to some of their pranks, Bob himself seems to have done all right out of the 'young gentlemen' of his waiting days in the early sixties: 'After their club dinners they'd lock me in the room with them and I had to tell jokes. The problem was some of the chaps went to, say, the rugby, hockey and soccer dinners, so I had to vary my act accordingly. At the end of the evening, I used to transport home several large cigars for my efforts – which my father enjoyed.'

Such a background of happy experiences goes a long way to explaining why 'Page the Wage', as Bob is known to the rest of the staff, is so content in his niche: 'Industry is a rat-race, where college life is easy-going. We haven't got big time limits or profit margins to worry about. I have to run to a budget, but it just about evens out. In industry it's a case of making money or you're out. But this is a good life, with good holidays, and money's not everything nowadays.'

Brian Barber, just a couple of years older than Bob, came to Sidney Sussex in search of job satisfaction too. He runs a staff of about a dozen in the college kitchens and has a high reputation with both the students and Fellows for his personal touch which includes catering, for example, for vegetarians and in some cases personal diets. He saw his move like this: 'After eleven years at Churchill, I'd worked my way up from pastry chef to head chef. I felt that Sidney offered me more in job satisfaction than Churchill could. Here I am my own boss, in a manner of speaking, with the one Bursar in charge of me. Churchill was bigger and more of a commercial set-up, so doing the dinners and feasts here is more satisfying. On the other hand I did bring in a self-service system for Hall meals. It meant we could offer the students more choice and at the same time cut our costs and labour charges. But we've got a good relationship going with the undergraduates, we're like a big family, I suppose. They're growing up and college life is part of it. Anyway, they never interfere with the kitchen side – they know where their bread's buttered!' Obviously there can be no suggestion these days that college staff go in awe of the young ladies and gentlemen.

Only the scholars among the undergraduates are invited to join the Fellows and college guests at the Foundation Feast in March, one of the four great feasts of the college year that put to the test the skills of Brian Barber and his team. This year as usual preparations for the Saturday evening began in the kitchens in mid-week. The menu had already been agreed with the Bursar, who had checked the French translation. Now Brian was phoning through his order to the family butcher who supplies his meat, and dashing over to the market to supplement an order with his supplier there for fruit and vegetables. Down in the wine cellars beneath the Great Hall, Albert Flack, the buttery manager, stock book in one hand, inspection lamp in the other, sought out the wines listed down the side of the menu by the Bursar. Upstairs in the strongroom he checked out and rubbed over the silver, cutlery and candlesticks, rose-bowls and an exquisite steeple cup, centre-piece for the high table.

By Friday the kitchen staff were gutting a pile of whole salmon and poaching the pears, with Brian and Michael, the second chef, periodically checking progress on the rest of their preparations. That day too there was the normal self-service lunch and evening meal to contend with. On Saturday morning the bread rolls were made, the poached salmon was dressed, the pears decorated and the vegetable dishes prepared. By mid-afternoon as the pressure eased the team were slipping off one by one into their rest-room next door for a quick cigarette and a swallow or two of their free beer ration. In the meantime, the buttery staff had laid out with precision the one hundred place settings, cutlery, cruets, wine glasses, menus and rolled napkins, each with a bread roll tucked in the top.

From her massive portrait above the high table, Lady Frances Sidney, Countess of Sussex, looked down on the sparkle of glass and silver set out for her Foundation Feast, *in piam memoriam fundactricis nostrae*. And in the kitchens by 7.30 pm, when the Master in scarlet gown led the College and its guests into the Hall, the full menu stood ready, worthy of its formal description:

	MENU
Puligny	Saumon Froid
Montrachet 1973	
	————
	Petite Marmite
	————
Ch. Guionne	Carottes à la Favorite
1970	
	————
Volnay	Filet de Boeuf à la Richelieu
1969	Pommes de Terre Chateaux
Veuve Clicquot	Aubergines Carlton
Brut 1970	Choux Braisés
	————
	Poires d'Arenberg
	————
	Beurreck à la Turque
	————
Ch. Calon Segur	Dessert
1966	
Ch. Guiraud 1967	————
Graham 1960	Café

In the manner of kitchen staff from time out of mind, those of the Sidney team who felt like it tucked into the same food and wine as the big-wigs that night. There was just the faintest flicker of disappointment at the number of guests who seemed unable to do justice to their best dishes, especially the *filet de boeuf*, but perhaps the reward now, as in the old days, lies in showing off your capabilities.

Talk of the 1980 Foundation Feast brought back a flood of memories to Harry Littlechild: 'They always had oysters to start with at Feast. Then they'd have a choice of two starters after that, then a choice of two fish and a choice of two soups. After that they'd have an entrée, a joint, sorbet, game, a choice of sweets, hot or cold, savoury, dessert, and all the best wines of course. In fact when I left college in 1974 they were just finishing the Taylor '25 and '27 which my original Steward bought. Many years later, at the last Feast he came to – he'd left by then – when he saw that the Taylor was on the menu, he said to me, "How much do you think I paid for those Harry?" I said, "I've no idea". He said, "Three and sixpence a bottle!"'

In Harry's day the Fellows had their favourite dishes which were asked for again and again. One he remembers especially was the 'boudin of whiting': 'It was whiting mixed with soaked bread and pounded up in a mortar. Then it was put in a mould and hollowed out in the middle. The middle was filled with oysters, crayfish, prawns and crab. Then it was sealed off and done in the bain marie. It wasn't allowed to boil – if it boiled, it blew. So you just kept it on the simmer in the oven.'

To Harry, eating on that scale was not gourmandising for the sake of it: 'You've got to remember that eating in those days was part of your education. This was one thing they came up for. I always remember one father saying to me that his son had come up here to be educated in how to eat.'

Harry Littlechild is one of Cambridge's best examples of how the old term 'college servant' all too often appeared to undervalue the man. As well as contributing considerably to the life of Sidney Sussex College over fifty years, Harry received a great deal of his own 'education' there, and went on to make wide-spread use of his new-found abilities. Reminiscing in the almost collegiate atmosphere of his panelled sitting room, Harry told us modestly about his many activities. For twelve years he sent apprentices to the Royal Household, he founded the Kitchen Manager's Association to work for common conditions of service within the colleges, and played a large part in organising inter-collegiate sport for college servants as Secretary of the College Servants' Club. Now, in retirement, he is busier than ever as Secretary of the Chefs' Association of Great Britain. Outside college life he focused his energy and organising abilities on the village of Cottenham, six miles north of Cambridge, where he had gone to live when he married in the late thirties. Apart from becoming a local councillor he turned his attention to the sports and social life of the village when he came out of the forces: 'When I came back to the village here to live, they couldn't find a secretary for the football club. I happened to be at the annual general meeting and somebody suggested me. Eventually I took on the cricket as well as the football, until I married the two clubs together, and then I re-formed the tennis club. From there we thought we'd like some premises, so we went round the village and got some interest-free loans from various people to build ourselves a club-room. It's very pleasing to see it flourishing.'

The 'club-room' now has grown into a full-scale sports and social club with playing fields and changing rooms, kitchen, spacious games room and club bar, where Harry can be found several times a week drinking his Scotch or pint of mild. When we joined him there he had just been invited to continue once again as Club President. 'I don't mind if that's what they want,' he said.

In this world Harry's role is the nearest thing to Master. Perhaps his memoirs when they are finished will shed light on some extra-mural influences of the colleges as yet undocumented.

Kersey

'You must live as if you were going to die tomorrow, but farm as though you were going to live forever.'

When Domesday book was compiled in 1086, Suffolk was the most densely populated part of England. Even after centuries of invasion and destruction its society was surprisingly settled – more than one third of the freemen of England listed appear to have lived in Suffolk. In an agrarian society the majority of these would have exercised their independence as yeoman farmers.

Central Suffolk is rich farming land, its alluvial deposits of boulder clay marking the southernmost limit of the ice-sheets of the Great Ice Age. This seemed the area to look for today's yeoman farmers, the inheritors of more than two thousand years of continuous agriculture and of an unbroken tradition of independence. It contrasts sharply with the areas to the north where for centuries there have been large manorial estates, and now there are insurance companies, pension funds and foreign investors who have created the vast 'prairies' that we regard as typical of East Anglia. Central, or 'High', Suffolk, is an area where change has come more slowly, and though today's farming units are vastly larger than their medieval counterparts, the predominant patterns of family land-ownership and employment date back for centuries.

If you approach the village of Kersey from the west in high summer through hedgeless fields of waving corn, you will stumble on a scene which, like so many of Suffolk's village streets, could be mistaken for a Hollywood film producer's dream. An irregular collection of pastel-coloured stone and timber cottages lead steeply down to a ford where constantly parading ducks hold up the occasional cars and tractors, and then even more steeply up again to the flint-walled tower and buttresses of St Mary's Church. The church now seems huge for so small a village, but it was built by the wool barons in the 1300s when Kersey was one of the largest settlements in Suffolk. Woollen cloth was then the principal source of England's wealth, and the village street would have echoed to the clatter of hundreds of looms. Even though it is centuries since the woollen trade moved on to Yorkshire, it is a past the tourist can easily envisage as he visits the church, photographs fourteenth-century cottages, calls in at the half-timbered Bell Inn just above the ford for morning coffee, lunch or dinner, and buys a souvenir from the pub's vast collection of corn dollies. Agricultural traditions on the other hand continue unbroken in these parts, but as fields show little of their past compared with buildings, the casual observer is unlikely to see anything remarkable in the 'working farms' which surround the village.

One of these is West Sampson Hall, home for generations of the Partridge family, and we began our film there on a dull November morning in 1977. The rambling, stuccoed farmhouse was half-way through a re-paint, a job forgotten earlier in the year at the onset of a busy season, like the Jubilee Union Jack still tied to the gate-post. In the farmhouse kitchen thirteen-year-old Kate Partridge was showing more concern for the fortunes of Ipswich Town than the wonders of nature.

Out in the fields, though, the pattern was more familiar to the romantically-minded. As early mist and light rain gave way to yellow autumn sunshine, two tractors worked rhythmically. Jim Baalham was ploughing in the stubble ready for the new season, his son Keith following a field or so behind with the disc harrow; Frank and Kenny Frost stooped side by side to pull and top the mangold crop by hand; George Hills, who has worked now for four generations of Partridges, was alone in the cabbage field, cutting the hearts to produce seed, one of the farm's specialities; Stan Norman loaded sugar beet, one of Suffolk's biggest crops these days, into a lorry; and Jimmy Pryke, fourth generation of his family to work on this farm, helped in a routine check of the sheep for minor ailments, working alongside Ivan Richardson, the young shepherd who comes of a long line of local families.

Over the next ten months these six hundred and sixty rich acres would provide crops of wheat, barley, maize, sugar beet, cabbage and parsnip seed, and the white clover seed that was first developed by John Partridge's father. In the course of the year calves would be fattened, lambs born and raised, hay cut and stored, and John Partridge, his sons and their ten or eleven workers would build up to the almost orgiastic work-load of the grain harvest.

John Partridge, a 'dirty boots' farmer

During the quieter winter months John Partridge is able to indulge his passion for the breeding of pedigree Suffolk sheep. January is lambing time, and for the most part ewes seem to prefer to give birth during the hours of darkness, so when we returned to the farm, we found John and young Kate, who is as keen on farming as her older brothers, standing in the cold moonlight in the deep litter of an enclosed stockyard. The pregnant ewes, mostly standing, were restless, their breath white in the light of John's torch. Generally ewes need little or no assistance with the birth of their lambs, but father and

West Sampson Hall Farm

daughter made frequent visits to the yard to watch for the telltale signs of a ewe about to give birth as it crept away to find a dark corner in one of the open stalls. After a while, if developments seemed too slow, John would move in, gently pull the sheep to the ground and, while Kate held its head with her knee on its forequarter, he would manipulate a tiny head or a twisted leg until the sheep, by its own efforts, gave birth. John must have seen this event many dozens of times before but there was still pleasure in his face as he watched, and saw the wet little bundle bleat within seconds and stand to suckle vigorously within minutes.

Later, as we warmed ourselves by the fire, John Partridge sat back in an armchair and showed us a family history compiled by his grandfather's cousin in 1937, a history of men once referred to as 'the aristocracy of the soil', the yeomen farmers of England. The Partridges can trace their ancestry back to the fifteenth century in this area of

'High' Suffolk, and John Partridge is the fourth generation to live at the West Sampson Hall farm itself, though even as the eldest son of his father, he did not inherit the farm in the straightforward manner which is usual elsewhere.

The inheritance patterns of Suffolk were largely established by the Frieslanders who settled there in the sixth century. They favoured partial inheritance by all the children, rather than primogeniture, the inheritance of everything by the eldest. This led to land being split into many smaller units, and was directly responsible for the large number of independent yeoman farmers in Suffolk recorded in Domesday Book.

The system still applies in principle today, so at fifty-five, John Partridge finds he has problems on a larger scale than previous generations. Besides having three daughters, Barbara married and living abroad, and Mary living and working in Ipswich, as well as Kate, John and his wife Naomi have four sons whose future has to be considered. John sees the problem in its historical perspective: 'The idea of the yeoman was to give all his sons a reasonably equal chance of a start in life. My father helped his other sons quite a lot and this farm had to pay for it. I've only just finished paying for my father starting off my younger brothers.'

At the beginning of 1978 with three sons in their twenties and a fourth still at school John was already thinking about working out that problem all over again, although a good deal still depended on his sons' own intentions. At twenty-six, Robert, the eldest, married with a young son, was already established in Bridges Farm, a mile away from the home farm, in effect managing the day-to-day running of the whole unit. Tim, aged twenty-four, and to his father 'the most natural farmer of them all' was living at home, sharing the responsibilities with Robert, though in more direct contact with the actual 'stuff' of growing and rearing. Twenty-one-year-old Peter was less sure about a future in farming. He was living in a caravan next to a derelict cottage he was restoring with his girl-friend Sal, while he thought it out. Chris, the youngest, still had a few years to go at school.

John chewed on some of the options and showed how they related to a complicated past: 'It's quite possible two of them could stay on this farm. We could buy a little more land, then split the farm, or they could work in together. Actually at the moment we're hoping to buy back part of the farm that my grandfather left to his daughter who's now died. My father left one field of this farm to another of his sons, and we've now bought that back. That makes three times our family has bought that field. My grandfather bought it and left it to one of his other sons, my father bought it off him and left it to one of my brothers and now we've bought it off him. So things are a little fairer than you might have thought. The eldest son doesn't take the lot in our family. If he wants it, he has to buy it back off his brothers and sisters.'

For all these limitations to being the eldest son, Robert seems to have stepped easily into his supervisory role. There is a quiet confidence in the separate life style he has established for himself with his French wife at Bridges Farm, a semi-proprietorial air even in the way he drives the old Land Rover. He sipped a glass of Pernod and reflected on his own situation: 'I think subconsciously I always wanted to be a farmer. Even though I tried out alternatives like going off to France at one stage, the first family I came across happened to be in agriculture. I got involved with the farm, took an interest in what was going on, married one of the farmer's daughters and here we are back again!'

From most people's point of view Robert would seem to have it made, sitting as he does on a square mile of land worth a fortune, if it were to be sold off. Naturally enough Robert is extremely reluctant to look at the family's inheritance that way, but a period away from the influence of his parents at agricultural college as well as in France, undoubtedly gave him a broader perspective on the problems of the future: 'To start with my choice of family size will definitely be smaller. My father's father was able, because land was cheaper in those days, if not to buy a farm for his sons, then at least to set them up in farming. Now it's out of the question. With land at £1000 to £2000 an acre it's very difficult for a farmer to recoup that sort of money in a generation.'

At the same time, with six hundred and sixty acres at those prices the Partridges would seem to be pretty well off, but Robert quickly dispels that idea: 'We're as rich as the money we earn, not as the capital we've got invested. And you'll never find much money in my pockets!'

Certainly there are no expensive cars or other obvious signs of wealth about the farm, and the social pleasures that Robert and his brothers enjoy tend to be rooted in the countryside and relatively

1 Market Place, Dudley

2 Yorkshire team plays an end-of-season benefit match at Saddleworth

5 The outer harbour, Whitby, with St Mary's Church and the abbey on the skyline

3 & 4 *Opposite*: Paintings from the Ashington Group: *above: North School Corner* by Oliver Kilbourn; *below, Ashington Colliery 1936* by Harry Wilson

6 King George's Dock, Hull

7 Sidney Sussex College, Cambridge: Fellows, Scholars and guests at the
Foundation Feast, 1980

8 Kersey village from the steps of St Mary's Church

9 & 10 *Above*, St George's Church, Portland; *below*, Terry and Dane Gould splitting a block by feathering

11 & 12 *Above*, One of Laura's paintings of engine houses; *below*, John and Laura Rowe at Botallack Cliffs

13 The post office in the square, Guiting Power

inexpensive. Apart from his love of fishing, Robert will often join a group of other young farmers from the district for a pheasant shoot during the season. On these informal social occasions there is a distinctly period quality about the nips from the hip flasks, the natty headgear, the earnest talk about dogs, and the banter about each other's performance. Robert is sensitive to criticism of the shoots and sees them in their context as part of the actual farming process: 'I've had dogs and carried guns since I was big enough to walk. Most farmers shoot in the first instance because they have to – we have to shoot rabbits and pigeons to preserve the crops. In January and February a flock of pigeons descending every day will polish off a five-acre field of cabbages like locusts. So we get good at it, and driven pheasants are slightly more difficult to shoot than either rabbits or pigeons. But I get cagey about this blood sports thing, because I firmly believe that if farmers didn't shoot or were not allowed to, wildlife in this country, apart from game, would be in a pretty poor state.' Since most farmers, Robert believes, are conservationists in their own interests, they will automatically tend to maintain and better the countryside.

The shoot too is perhaps the farmer's only chance to take a proper look at the countryside they live in: 'Hordes of people come out from towns to look at the countryside, and the people who live in the country wonder what they're doing, because when you're working in the countryside all the time, it's difficult to see it in the same light. When we're out shooting, it's maybe the only chance we have to stand back and take it in. And besides that, it's one of the only opportunities we get to walk over other people's farms and cast an eye to what they're doing!'

With his curly black beard and broad shoulders, and maroon boiler-suit worn almost constantly over varying numbers of sweaters, Tim Partridge is the 'dirty hands' farmer of the family, totally committed to a farming career. From the time he was a tiny boy, his father says, no one could have imagined him doing anything else. Nor could we as we followed him round barns and stockyards, trying to get a word in. Tim himself never had any doubts either: 'If we hadn't had the land or if I couldn't have gone into farming for some other reason, obviously I would have done something else. But it would probably have been connected with agriculture or the countryside. I definitely couldn't have sat in an office or have been anything like an accountant.

I just like being in the country. Your job's on your doorstep, so you don't have to get up and spend an hour or two travelling every day. There's only five or six days a year when it's too rough to work and anyway you dress up when it's cold and strip off when it's warm. You may be on call twenty-four hours a day, but I wouldn't do anything else.'

Tim's dedication to farming showed his future was already determined, even without his father's commitment to the yeoman system of split inheritance, but for Peter, third of the sons, there was less certainty. He, like Robert, had long ago worked out that times had changed a great deal since his grandfather managed to set up his father and two uncles in farming: 'I suppose when I was about twelve or thirteen I decided that the farm really was not big enough to support the three oldest sons, so I decided, sort of sub-consciously I suppose, that farming was not for me. I've enjoyed working on the farm as such since I left college, but I definitely don't want to stay here as a worker, or as part of what you might call the managerial staff either, because I just don't think the farm is profitable enough to set all three of us up in farming. So really I've got to do something else.'

For the time being though, Peter's main preoccupation was the completion of Warrener's Cottage, unoccupied for twenty-one years and still without light or water. Whatever his eventual decision about farming, as he pointed out himself, he was unlikely to leave the area for some considerable time, since the grants he and Sal had obtained on the cottage only six miles from Kersey committed them to living there for at least five years. So even though his mother would clearly have been happier to see him at home rather than roughing it in a caravan with his girlfriend, the family were leaving it to Peter to work out his own ideas and make the next move. At the same time they obviously hoped that the Suffolk accent would eventually prove more durable than the shoulder-length hair or the hippy headband.

Every Thursday one end of the huge kitchen table at West Sampson Hall is covered with books, papers and a calculator, as the 'farm secretary', Naomi Partridge, tackles the wages, bills, VAT and ever increasing variety of forms that have to be passed on to the accountants. Mrs Partridge began her working life in the offices of a local miller and merchant so it was no great difficulty to her to add the role of secretary to those of mother, caterer and discreet general manager of household affairs. She denies taking any direct part in the for-

Family tea at West Sampson Hall Farm. Seated, *left to right*: Tim, Chris, Kate, Robert and Peter. John and Naomi are standing behind their children

mulation of farm policy, but since most decisions emerge out of a succession of tea-table conferences, she is usually closely involved. In reflective moments her sons acknowledge that it is mother who keeps all of them on their toes.

As the sons take on more and more of the day-to-day running of the farm, John Partridge is able to devote more of his time to the things he positively enjoys. Specifically this means the raising of his pedigree Suffolk sheep, which as Robert pointed out are more of a hobby than a money-maker. Enjoyable or not, sheep mean a lot of work, especially at lambing-time, and the farm employs a full-time shepherd.

Ivan Richardson is twenty-eight, and his local roots are every bit as well-founded as the Partridges. With his dark features and strong cheekbones it comes as no surprise that there is gypsy blood on one side of his family. The other side were thatchers. He comes of the Richardsons and Riddlestones of nearby Polstead. These two families, like many others in Suffolk, have intermarried down the generations, and as John Partridge put it with a grin: 'They're perhaps

Manor Farm, one of the tied cottages, once the home of John and his family, now occupied by the Baalhams

even more pure-bred stock than our family. Some of them haven't got as many great-grandfathers as most people, but it doesn't seem to have done them any harm.'

John recalled the almost casual way in which Ivan came to join him: 'His father was doing contract agricultural work, but one of his grandfathers had been a shepherd. A few years ago he came over here and said "Can I look at the sheep?" I said of course he could look at the sheep. So he looked at the sheep, and then he said, "Can I come and help for a week at lambing time?" I said yes, jolly good. So he came and helped, and then he went off and helped somebody else. Then when he heard our old shepherd was ill, he came back to help out and he's been here on and off ever since.'

For his age Ivan is a surprisingly old-fashioned and contented farm-hand. He works hard at being relaxed, and there is a studied casualness about the battered trilby, the coloured neckerchief and the old greatcoat tied at the waist with twine that he flings off at the end of a wet and windy day tramping the fields, before getting his feet up on the stove of one of the Partridges' tied cottages. The thatched cottage

Two more tied cottages – the home of Ivan Richardson, the shepherd, is on the left

is neat and full of souvenirs of visits to stately homes, a pastime he shares with his young London wife who works as a doctor's receptionist in Hadleigh, the nearest town. He expressed satisfaction rather than enthusiasm about his work: 'It's a wet and cold job, but it's got its good points. You're outside in the fresh air, you live almost on your work and to a certain extent you're your own boss. If I want to get up at four in the morning and set my folds to help myself forward for the weekend, then I do, so I can have a freer weekend. I know there are other jobs where there's more money to start with, but you see, money doesn't mean anything to me. I know you've got to have a certain amount of money, but as they say, you can't buy happiness, that comes with contentment. If you're contented, you're happy, and that's it.'

To Ivan Richardson the much-criticised tied cottage system obviously provides a part of his contentment: 'How else could my wife and I have got a house without a mortgage hanging over our heads?' Certainly there were no grouses from Jim Baalham, Frank Frost and the half-dozen or so other workers who live in the farm's tied cottages.

John Partridge feels quite strongly about the criticism: 'I think there's a lot of rubbish talked about tied cottages. If you go and ask our chaps if they'd rather go and live in a council house and pay about £4 or £5 rent and rates, instead of living rent and rates free, I think I know what answer they'd give you.'

As so often of course, the working of such a system depends heavily on who the boss is, and in the case of John Partridge his strong religious principles give him a sense of commitment to his long-standing workers: 'Generally it's my policy that if a man has worked for us for a number of years, then he deserves to carry on in his cottage in his retirement, just as I hope to have somewhere not far away to live when I retire.'

John Partridge is an active member of the United Reformed Church and an upholder of the strong Suffolk tradition of non-conformity. He still preaches regularly in the small clapboard chapel built on the farm by his father. His wife plays the harmonium for the singing from the Sankey hymn book, and their younger children, Chris and Kate, sit on the hard benches among a congregation of relatives and workers as John delivers his sermon in plain down-to-earth language that underlines his conviction. He explained to us, not without humour, what his faith means to him: 'To me it's the essence of life. I know you think that perhaps the sheep are, but basically the Christian religion is what makes me tick. In farming we can think we are working with God in nature. "We plough the fields and scatter the good seed on the land," as the hymn says, "but it is fed and watered by God's almighty hand."'

And even Robert, who is unlikely to be seen in chapel these days, felt a sense of mystery about his relationship with the land: 'There's definitely something magic about planting things and seeing them grow, isn't there? I can't see much point in trying to find something more mystic than that, but that in itself is quite something.'

That year, as every year, the magic worked and the crops grew, but in other ways 1978 proved to be a year of change on the Partridge Farm. By the time we made our final trip to Kersey in August for the grain harvest, Tim had married Pat Holland, one of two daughters of a farmer at Lavenham, ten miles away, and had accepted an offer to go into partnership with her father on their five-hundred-acre farm. It was not such a complex unit as the Partridge farm, and he was already making plans to compensate for the reduction of variety in his farming life, by 'borrowing' one or two of the seed-growing specialities from his home farm. At the same time he realised the move would probably make things easier back at home: 'Robert and I had just been going on rather presuming that we would work the farm together, and with six hundred acres that's just about possible. It will probably be more of an advantage to future generations than at the moment, but it does mean now that someone younger from further down the family will have more of a chance to step in if they want to.'

Obviously he meant Peter, but Peter himself was not rushing into any swift decisions: 'Strangely enough, Tim's moving away doesn't seem to have made that much difference to me. Rob's taken on a lot more responsibility for things, but as far as I'm concerned it doesn't really affect the fact that I decided when I was at school that I wasn't going to be part of the farm. So all along I haven't been as involved in the farm as the others. At the moment I'm spending most of my spare time doing up the house and that's the most important thing to me. When that's done, I'll sort out where I go from there.'

Robert was optimistic that Tim's move would be good for everyone: 'It came as a bit of a surprise, but I think it is the best thing Tim could have done. And obviously it gives me more chance to do the things I want to do, to farm the way I want to farm without having to compromise with Tim. I think it may take Pete a year or two before he takes things more seriously, because he needs to see a few seasons come and go while he's really involved in it to realise, for example, the urgency of seasonal things. I hope Tim's moving out will change the way he looks at it because I get on very, very well with Pete, probably because I went through the same kind of semi-rebellion. If he did change his mind and want to come in with me on the business, I'd be very happy about it. But it's entirely up to him.'

It was apparent that Robert had been gradually putting his mark on the farm for some time, and that now he was beginning to flex his muscles on specific issues: 'On our farm at present every single half-acre is farmed, there's no woodland at all, but just recently I've been given the go-ahead by the powers that be to plant a three-acre piece down behind my house. This is something I've always wanted to do.'

'The powers that be', Robert explained, still meant his father, and in spite of his keenness to express himself by developing the farm his way, he was anxious not to appear too thrusting: 'I am not hoping the day will rush on me when the final decision-making is mine. I don't

Pedigree Suffolk sheep

want to put the day off but there's no point in grabbing at it, because at the moment I don't want to make any sweeping changes. You see, I'm already imagining myself in my father's situation. I often do that. He really enjoys looking after sheep. Now I would like to try to do the things he's *had* to do all his life, so that he can spend more time doing what he enjoys. I'm never going to tell my father he can't have sheep. That would be like my son Lawrence telling me that I couldn't shoot, and there's no way my son is going to do that!'

Though John Partridge himself would prefer his sons not to shoot, and would no doubt be pleased to see them back in chapel, it is obvious that the father's general philosophy of life has greatly influenced the sons. There is a natural morality in their relationship with each other, with their workers and even in their attitude to the land they have inherited. Without any of the fashionable or fanciful talk about 'organic farming' John described himself as 'a sort of natural farmer' and explained simply: 'We feel a responsibility towards the actual land itself, and it's not a romantic attitude, we really do. We like to keep the land in good heart, as we call it. We use quite a lot of farmyard manure, and grow grass and clover that we graze for three or four years and then plough back in to keep up the fertility of the soil. You've got to know your land and work with it, not against it, but that's the sort of thing you pick up in a few years – you don't need generations for that.' Then suddenly and unexpectedly his eyes misted over and he said: 'It's a nice thought though, that your great-grandfather farmed the same land . . .'

Robert is equally clear about the values of their kind of farming and emphatically rejects the temptations of a flashier life-style: 'It's all a question of the quality of life, isn't it? I mean if this farm made lots of money, which it could, and I had a bigger salary, I'd then go about spending that money trying to buy back those things I'd destroyed in making the money. I really can't see the point because I enjoy doing the things I do. I like this area, the fields, the farm itself. I like all the trees on the farm, and I wouldn't want to bulldoze them all out just to make a few more pounds.'

At harvest time though, philosophy took second place to practicality as the present generations pulled together to bring in the grain. Tim came back from Lavenham to help out driving the straw baler, Robert was using fruity language about the teething troubles of a brand-new combine harvester, and Peter was driving the grain truck backwards and forwards from cornfield to grain store as though he had never had second thoughts about farming. Robert and Jim Baalham took turns on the combine to keep the machines going most of the hours of day and night.

When the sun shines, this can be a very satisfying time of year for the farmer, and John Partridge seemed in optimistic mood as, after a few hectic days, he made his way back to the farmhouse down the avenue of young oaks in his front meadow: 'We planted these oaks to mark one hundred years of the family being on this farm. That was almost twenty-five years ago now. So I'm hoping that in another hundred years the family will still be here, and I think it's quite likely now, with grandchildren coming on.'

Roman Road, Bow

*'I think it's given me more satisfaction than any other job. I've had
other jobs where I thought I was enjoying it, but come Monday morning
I'd say, "Christ, here we go again!" But not with this job; I'm always
quite happy to go.'*

The visitor in search of Cockneyland soon discovers that a journey to
the East End of London today can be a depressing experience. Images
of pearly kings and queens and the gaiety of music hall fade away as he
wanders from Bermondsey to Rotherhithe and the Surrey Docks area
south of the river. Odd spots of colour remain along the Rotherhithe
waterfront and river traffic is still busy, but the Surrey Docks, once
the biggest commercial timber docks in the world, with names like
Greenland, Quebec and Russia, are now derelict and weed-grown.

North of the river in Millwall too the docks, referred to now as 'the
upper docks', are doomed as more and more traffic moves down-river
to Tilbury. A bus-ride from Whitechapel reveals all too many peeling
rows of boarded-up houses punctuating the deserts between tower
blocks. In the area including Bow, Stepney, Limehouse and Poplar,
all part now of the London Borough of Tower Hamlets, there is less
and less visual evidence of the trades and professions of the past. Even
the rag trade sweatshops are fewer and more isolated than formerly,
and it will be several generations before the immigrant Asians who
run most of them now are as accepted as the Jews who came before
them, or the Huguenots before that. Altogether the area reveals a lack
of community focus or identity.

The exception comes as a vigorous, blinding flash of old London
in the heart of Tower Hamlets. The Roman Road street market at
Bow bursts into life on Tuesdays, Thursdays and especially Saturdays. Apart from Petticoat Lane – which many East Enders now
regard as just a tourist attraction – Roman Road is the only full-scale
street market left in the East End.

'The Roman', as the two hundred-odd stallholders affectionately
call it, lies about three miles as the crow flies east of St Paul's. The

Saturday market day early in 1980

tenants on top of Lefevre Walk flats at the end of Roman Road look down on what might be the permanent back-lot of a film studio, one old street in a sea of modern blocks. Even on non-market days it still retains its identity as an old-style shopping street with rows of small shops, the odd bank and building society, and Woolworths a few shop-fronts wide. Two eel and pie shops look unchanged since the 1940s, and every day the fruit and vegetable boys, descendants of the old costermongers, are on most street corners proclaiming their wares fresh from Spitalfields just down the road. Though the goods on sale are far from tatty, prices in the shops and on the stalls are uniformly

Roman Road, Bow 139

lower than elsewhere. The attraction of Roman Road in an area where poverty is far from dead and unemployment is high and rising is value for money. The population of Tower Hamlets has dropped twenty-five per cent in ten years in spite of the Borough accepting council tenants from other parts of London and taking more than its share of homeless people. Many of those who left were the younger skilled workers, but the market continues to thrive because those who stayed need a bargain, and many of those who left come back regularly for the square deal they remember. Bargain hunting up and down the road has been the appeal of street markets from the beginning.

Just when the Roman Road market began became a subject for debate early in 1980. For some years in the winter months between Christmas and Easter when business is slackest, the Roman Road Traders' Association has been developing its Winter Shopping Festival, not only to drum up trade, but also to raise money for local charities. The 1980 festival was to be a bigger event than previously, so as an aid to publicity, it was decided that this year might well be the hundred and fiftieth anniversary of the start of Roman Road market. Historians, amateur and otherwise, began burrowing for the truth, but soon discovered that the history of the market was far from exactly recorded. There was no market charter to be found, and if the Romans gave us London, they certainly did not leave us Roman Road. In 1843 it was a cart track known as Green Street, when records indicate some market dealings, probably in cattle, although between 1830 and 1840 the areas of Bow, Bromley, Poplar, Limehouse and Mile End were known for market gardening. Before the end of the 1840s the road had been constructed, and the houses built by 1865 were joined by shops soon afterwards. Certainly the market was going strong by 1888 when a police threat to remove the stalls provoked a reaction whose echo has been heard again in recent years.

In 1888 handbills were distributed urging all tradesmen and cos-termongers to rally to 'A Monster Meeting' at the 'Hand and Flower'. In the last few years, suggestions by local authority planners of a 're-organisation' of the market have led to the matter being dealt with in gentlemanly debate between council and traders. Harry da Costa, chairman of the Traders' Association, regularly leads a small del-egation to the Tower Hamlets council offices for discussions with the ponderously-titled Assistant Director of Community Services, Public Protection and Co-ordination, Mr Lockwood, and his deputy Mr

Moss, Markets and Consumer Protection Officer. In spite of the off-putting titles, personal representation seems to work, and the market continues in its original form. Even so it is doubtful whether Harry and his fellow traders could make a better case for the market than was spelt out by the nine hundred and fifty signatories to the petition of 1888:

> The stalls form a cheap market for the benefit of the neighbourhood and working classes. If they are removed, it will cause considerable inconvenience to many people as they would have to travel some distance to find a similar market where they could purchase their daily requirements.

The local population still pours down from their flats and maisonettes on market days, and now that it is not the problem 'to travel some distance' that it was in 1888, those whose homes were displaced by the flats come back from all over London and beyond. Some come looking only for bargains, but others born locally journey back from impersonal suburbs eager to wallow in nostalgia. They can be found every Thursday and Saturday morning crammed into Kelly's eel and pie shop, women of all ages, their children and a few old men. From early morning Mrs Beatrice Kingdon and her daughter Sue, who gave up teaching to come back into the business, are hard at work with their staff of eight baking anything up to fourteen hundred pies and preparing the mash and 'liquor' (parsley gravy). Behind the steamy windows bowls of jellied eels are laid out, ready for the rush at eleven o'clock. Eels are practically in the luxury class these days at 62p a portion, but the attraction of pie and mash at 36p will keep a queue outside the shop for two and a half hours, with many of the ladies carrying off bundles of pies and cartons of liquor to their friends and relatives as far afield as St Albans.

Kelly's eel and pie shop, like the coffee shop it originally was, has always had a trade built on the success of the market. Even these older shops are 'second generation' to the market, and job traditions among the market people are generally much older than among the shop-keepers. Perhaps the longest-lived job tradition in the market is that of costermonger. Henry Mayhew in *London Labour and the London Poor* (1861–2) said: 'they appear to be a distinct race, seldom associating with any other of the street-folks and being all known to each other.'

Kelly's, where old friends meet

About the time that Mayhew was writing of London's estimated thirty thousand costermongers Tom Old was setting up the Old family's first fruit and vegetable stall in Roman Road. Now various members of the family have four or five stalls in the market. Sixty-five-year-old Fred is in fruit, helped by his grandson Patrick, who some days runs his own clothes stall. Down the street past the stalls of Fred's cousin Reg and nephew Frank is one of the smartest vegetable pitches in the street. This is manned by brothers Alan and John Old, supervised from the steps of the van by their father George, Fred's brother.

At six o'clock on a thin March morning we found Fred and Patrick along the road at Spitalfields Market sniffing around the boxes of oranges and grapefruit at Glutman's stand. Fred, who seldom has his teeth in, produced a penknife, cut an orange in half and sucked it noisily. He is not much more than five feet tall, with flat cap and twinkling eyes, but he glowered up at a stocky fellow in sheepskin

'How about a bunch of bananas?' Fred Old at work

jacket when he found a bad grapefruit in the first crate he tried. The price dropped and the glower turned to a wink, but business is business even when the dealer is your son, Colin. Colin Old once had a stall 'down the Roman' like his father, but now feels he is doing better for himself among the dealers, even if he does have to start at three in the morning. Before Fred had completed his bartering, Colin's cousins John and Alan dropped by for a look over his onions and a rude word about the prices. Then, after a good-natured exchange, they were off with their van-load of sprouts and potatoes to their pitch and the early shoppers.

As they set out their stall, these two tough-looking Cockney lads demonstrated an almost delicate pride in making the most of their wares. A mound of sprouts became a perfect pyramid, each one that showed peeled down to its best layer, the whole edifice crowned by a few cut in two to show that quality was more than skin deep. The same went for carrots, parsnips, cauliflowers, all deftly trimmed and

Three generations of the Old family. *From left to right*: Frank Millie, his uncles George and Fred Old, on the right George's sons Alan and John, and between them Patrick Barrie, Fred's grandson

stacked to catch the eye in a market where there are plenty of other stalls to choose from. The exercise was obviously commercially as well as aesthetically successful since it is not unusual to see either Alan or John disappear mid-morning to Spitalfields for replacements.

They were taught the finer points of the trade by their father George. Now sixty-three and forced into partial retirement by a heart attack, he watched his sons at work, anxious not to interfere but obviously still nervous of their inexperience and at a loss for anything else to do. He has time to remember the days when no one could have afforded to sit back at his age: 'When I was a lad we lived in one of nine little cottages in Prince Albert's Avenue. Every house had mice and rats in them days. Once a week we used to go along the road here to Bow Baths with sixpence, a towel and bit of soap, and that was it. I wouldn't say "bad old days", just "hard old days". No one moved out of the street in them days. They all went and borrowed off one another and that created a bit of friendship. There's nothing like that today.'

Before the war almost all the traders lived 'just round the corner' from Roman Road, pushing their goods to and from the market on hand-barrows they kept at home. Most of those who were not bombed out moved away after the war as the housing was re-developed, with the result that the street traders are no longer the close fraternity that they were when George was a boy. That was also the time when the Old family spirit and enterprise came out at its strongest: 'When my father died, the family sort of collapsed. Myself and my brother had to go into a home, because we were the youngest. I had two other brothers and three sisters, and they all foraged for themselves. But one of my elder brothers carried on at the market when he was sixteen, and built the business up again. He'd go and buy a package of something for 7/6d and he'd double it. Get some more stuff, back to the market and double it again, until he built up a business good and properly. Just before the war he was employing fifteen to twenty barrow boys.'

The job is still hard but it has improved. George says: 'In the old days, make no mistake, it was back-breaking. Potatoes used to come in hundredweights, oranges used to be weighed in hundredweights, everything was like that. Now everything's a third of that weight and much cleaner.'

George has no regrets about the family tradition that drew him in, and his sons after him: 'We're not a family to be working indoors, or in factories. Even in a shop you daren't say a bad word to a customer, or you've lost him straightaway. On a stall you can tell one or two to hop it. They'll soon come back because they can see your goods all round. They go into a shop, they feel captured. On a stall they can walk round and still go away.'

It was largely force of circumstances that brought Alan and John Old in their mid-twenties to take over their father's stall. They had helped on the stall on Saturdays since they were six years old, but before their father's heart attack each had tried other jobs like engineering and driving. But when illness struck, there was no question of letting the old firm go. Both gave up their jobs and went full-time into the market. They show little regret. As Alan put it: 'I think it would drive me mad in a factory now. It was all right at the time, but now I've been out in the open the last two and a half years, I couldn't go back. The worst thing at first was getting up in a morning, but you get used to it. You just don't stay out so late of a night. It's your living, isn't it?'

Early on a market day, Brian Baker sets out his stalls

One of the first in the street each market-day morning is Brian
Baker. At about 7 am he and his boys can be heard before they are seen
pulling out the rows of traditionally-built stalls on their iron-clad,
wooden-spoked wheels. Well over a hundred will be set out on their
appropriate pitches by the time the traders begin to arrive. Hiring
out the trolleys is a thriving business for Brian Baker, although he
admits that some of his older customers still get their stalls at a weekly
rent quite ridiculously low for the 1980s. He maintains the stalls with
loving care in his workshop behind the billboards at one end of the
market, fighting a continual battle to keep up with vandals, regular
wear and tear, or the sheer age of the trolleys. Many of the parts are
obsolete, but Brian reckons to be able to repair or re-make any of
them. He only draws the line at making the wooden wheels from
scratch.

His hobby is training and showing cart horses, which brings back
family echoes of 1920 when his grandfather started the business:
'Grandfather was driving horse trams at the time and someone told
him there was a good living doing barrows. So he made his first one in
the basement and built things up from there.' He pointed to an old

hand-barrow across the yard: 'When I came down here just after the war, we had those and trestle stalls. There weren't so many four-wheeled trolleys then.'

Now fire regulations require that all the stalls should be readily movable, so trestle stalls disappeared in favour of the trolleys. Brian pointed out that the old iron-clad wheels roll easier than the newer rubber wheels which cost has forced him to introduce, but the stock of old wheels he has repaired and hidden away should enable him to maintain the market's old-fashioned mobility for many years yet. Long enough for his eight-year old son Terry, already happily slapping on paint in the yard, to take over from his father.

One of the oldest of the shops that grew up around the market is Cohens of Bow, men's and boys' outfitters. Between 1893 and 1901, when numbers of immigrant Jewish tailors were setting themselves up in the East End, the market doubled in size, to two hundred and three stalls. Wolf Cohen had arrived from Poland in the 1890s and began his working life in England with an East End clothes merchant. By 1904 he was ready to open his own shop in Roman Road. It was a converted house, with living quarters above and a kitchen in the basement. That shop was bombed in October 1940, but a large photograph of it, Wolf in the doorway, still hangs in the present chrome-fronted premises further up the street.

Running the business now is Wolf's son, Lew Cohen, about sixty, small, courteous and softly-spoken: 'In the beginning, with the help of one or two other people, my father produced made-to-measure suits. I remember when I first started in the shop our trading hours were nine in the morning till eight at night. Thursday was half-day, but the afternoon was taken up with buying, so you were lucky if you got home before six or seven in the evening. On Sundays we'd be open until two in the afternoon and at Christmas time it was nothing unusual for us to close at midnight. It was the same with the majority of shops.'

Many of the shopkeepers spread into the street by taking the stall in front of their shops. This served both to expand their space and to protect their windows from obstruction, but in Cohen's case the need to acquire the pitch out front went further: 'The stall used to sell offal, sheep's heads and the like. It was enough to put anyone off looking in our window, so when the old man died and the stall became vacant, we thought we'd better step in before something worse took its place.'

Wolf Cohen in the doorway of his original shop in 1904

Immaculately dressed in three-piece suit, Lew Cohen still knows his custom well enough to sell all the leading brands of jeans as well as fashionable lines in suits and separates. At the same time there is regret in his voice as he shows you the labels from Yugoslavia, Italy or Israel. 'British manufacturers would tell you where to go if you asked them to produce such well-finished suits at those prices,' he said.

Reluctantly he has had to accept that he cannot compete either, and he makes few suits to measure these days. Small wonder there is a strong air of nostalgia about as he recalls the days before the war:

'There was no fear of goods disappearing then, so things were hung up outside the shop. In those days of course this was a great naval nation, and little boys wore sailor suits. They sold at 4/11d and 5/6d, and made-to-measure three-piece suits were 21/- to 27/6d, as you can see here.' He pointed to the photograph where the prices were clearly visible.

The changes in the trade itself have obviously led Lew Cohen to be less concerned with the continuance of family tradition in the 'Roman' than the Old family: 'My father said to me that I *had* to go into his business. But to me in this day and age that's the wrong thing to say. My son, even to this day, doesn't know I was upset in the first instance that he didn't come into my business. But now of course I'm very pleased for him that he's made his own way in the world and is doing reasonably well.'

Although as one might expect a number of the market traders have Jewish backgrounds, it is surprising to discover how long some of their families have been in this country. Harry da Costa, chairman of the Traders' Association, is descended from seven Portuguese Jewish brothers who came to England four hundred and fifty years ago. Perhaps it is the closeness of Jewish family bonds that has kept him aware of those origins, but how many English families would not find at least one immigrant in the cupboard if they were able to trace their antecedents back to 1530? Naturally enough, Harry regards himself as English, and sees no significance in the Jewish origins of many market traders: 'Of course there are a lot of Jewish traders. There are also a lot of non-Jewish traders!'

As Harry admits, he is not hypocritical enough to pretend to be Orthodox since his best day's business is on Saturdays, and that goes for all the Jewish traders in Roman Road, but he keeps up his connections as a Batallion Sergeant Major in the Jewish Lads' and Girls' Brigade: 'I'm involved in that because I enjoy working with youth and I feel I'm doing some good. In all the years I've been associated with them, I've never known one of my boys or girls get into trouble with the police, or anyone else.'

Harry, now in his fifties, runs a lingerie stall with his wife, Marie. He was brought up in Benworth Street, just a few hundred yards from the 'Roman', into a family of market people, and has had a stall himself since he was demobbed in 1946. On the mantelpiece of his home in Gants Hill, Ilford, stands a pair of silver candlesticks pre-

Harry da Costa, chairman of the Traders' Association

sented to his parents as a wedding present in 1925 by the Roman Road and Old Ford Costermongers' Union. Harry's grandfather was chairman of that organisation, forerunner of the present Traders' Association.

Apart from one grandmother who was well known in Roman Road in 1938, Harry recalls he had 'four uncles, an aunt, three cousins, my mother, father and both grandfathers in the market business. My mother and aunt were in lingerie, the rest were job buyers.'

The art in being a job buyer lies in buying anything you think you can sell, so as a boy Harry's home became his training ground: 'When we lived in the East End, my father used the front room as a stock room and I saw all sorts of things in there. I can't remember anything my father didn't sell on a stall, from chocolates and cheese, to groceries, dresses and toys. Once he bought a load of chocolate marshmallows, and naturally myself, my brother and a few other kids raided the front room. We opened one box up and there were more worms than marshmallows. So all that lot went in the dustbin. There must have been three or four hundred pounds' worth, and in those days that was a heck of a lot of money. It's just one of the risks you take. The average job buyer will go into a factory and try to buy stuff at a ridiculous price. The owner of the factory is just as keen to get rid of his rubbish, so he'll try and catch you. It's dog eat dog.'

Apart from keeping an eye on unscrupulous suppliers, the job buyer may well need ingenuity to move the goods. After the war Harry picked up a load of barrage balloons and sold them as car covers: 'I think that's about the most peculiar line I've ever had. But they went – and at a good profit.'

To the casual observer the market trader's approach may seem easy come, easy go. Throw a load of nighties or junk jewellery on a barrow, do a bit of patter, then sit back and count the money. But Harry and his colleague-competitors need to be more precise about their business than that. 'You've only got to buy one bad lot for a large amount of money, and you're out of business,' says Harry.

The traders' exact sources may be a closely guarded secret, but the principles are common to all of them: 'Most of us buy from manufacturers, not from wholesalers. We buy direct, we buy clearing lines. Some of us even have stuff made, which again cuts out the margin of profit that the shop or the supermarket has to make, although if you work it out on a square footage basis, our overheads are almost as much as a shop's on a comparison of size. As far as stock is concerned, in the main we pay the same prices as shopkeepers do. But we can afford to sell at a lower price because we haven't got staff. We are usually a one-man business or perhaps a man and his wife, so we can afford to cut our prices considerably.'

But however calculated the approach, Harry is quick to point out that, 'If you want security, you don't go into the market.' At the same time his almost buccaneering approach to business suggests he positively enjoys the risks: 'Although I only sell lingerie, I will still go into a factory and buy a complete line – perhaps twenty or thirty dozen of an article – and, quite honestly, you never know until you get it on the stall if it's going to sell or not. Mostly I'm right, but occasionally I'm wrong. If I'm wrong, I cut my losses and get rid of them at any price. I have a sale to bring people in. All right, I might lose a hundred pounds, two hundred, but in the long run I'll make it up on something else.'

Lennie Sellick, in his early forties and on the next stall to Harry, is a new boy in the market. A few years ago he packed up his watchmaker's business and exchanged a life of quiet craftsmanship for the extrovert hustle of selling dress fabrics and the odd batch of nylon underskirts: 'The decision was to some extent financial. Repairing and selling watches wasn't too successful, so I tried to think of something else. We changed our shop to a dress shop, which my wife could run while I went to the markets. The first thing I tried to sell was jewellery, and I had a pantograph machine for engraving. After that I decided the markets were better than sitting there in a shop with a tiny eyeglass – I felt like an old man.

'I didn't originally do the job as I do it now. I'd just stand there like a lemon and not say a word to anybody. I think I'm basically shy anyway, but slowly you build up confidence in what you're doing and the customers start having confidence in you. I found it's a case of "Hello, love" instead of "Good morning, Madam." You're on top, they come to you. You have an immediate contact which you didn't have in the shop. If anybody came to you in the shop, you had to behave in a certain fashion, otherwise it didn't work. In the market I can say anything to some of the women. I do, and I get away with it. Try that in a shop and they'd be running for the police!'

At home in Chingford with his wife Noreen and twelve-year-old son Lawrence, talking quietly but incisively about his new business, Lennie seems hardly the same person as the wisecracking performer of the market. There he attacks the job with the gusto of a Ken Dodd or Les Dawson. To a lady who asks for a length of fabric, about two metres: 'Only in yards, love. I promised the judge I wouldn't do meters,' or of broderie anglaise: 'It's got to go – it's full of holes.'

To Lennie the job is all tied up with personal chemistry: 'If I go to work on any day and I just don't feel like it – say I have a hangover or something – it's just no good, I might just as well have stayed at home in bed. If I had a headache in the shop, it made no difference. They came to buy a watch, and they went out with one. But if I sit on the end of the stall with a big long face, it's no deal. I'm absolutely guaranteed to take no money. I suppose you've got to sell yourself to a certain extent.'

Though it seems he could sell furs in the tropics, Lennie insists that the 'Roman's' survival rests as much as anything else on a fair deal: 'I can honestly say that I've never ripped anybody off. It wouldn't work anyway. It's too open in a market. If they've got a complaint, for instance, they have to be dealt with, and I always turn it to my own advantage. Say somebody brings a piece of cloth back and says it's got

Lennie Sellick preparing for a wet day's work

a hole in it or a fault mark, I can make a tremendous show about it, either give them their money back or exchange it – and enjoy doing it. That way I win the others who are standing listening.'

Lennie's son, Lawrence, had been listening carefully, quiet for once, while we talked. Despite the obvious job satisfaction that market life has brought him, Lennie seems none too keen on seeing his son follow him on the stall: 'I think he would be better at it than I am because he's so outward going. He helps me on odd days now, but to be honest, I don't like him hanging around down there too often.

Besides, it's a very long day for a kid. But if he wants to do what I'm doing, fine. I really enjoy what I do. I don't care if it's raining, snowing or whatever, I'm still happy to go to work. I wouldn't like to retire at all, and in this job you don't have to. You are your own master. I don't believe in retirement. Anybody who works all their life and then, suddenly, they've got nothing to do, I think it's just crazy. You should draw a pension at twenty and start a job at sixty-five! But this job has given me more satisfaction than any other job. I've had other jobs where I thought I was enjoying it, but come Monday morning I'd say, "Christ, here we go again". But not with this job, I'm always quite happy to go.'

Like most of the regulars, Lennie works other markets than Roman Road to fill out the week, but all the traders share a preference for the traditional linear street market. If you ask why, Morrie Ness, friend and competitor of Harry da Costa in Roman Road, will point you a mile nearer the river to Chrisp Street in the Poplar end of Tower Hamlets: 'Chrisp Street was a wonderful market before the last war. It was even larger than this market then, and my father stood there for many years.' Then after the war it was 're-organised' on a square, a few dozen stalls clustered round a cramped brick arcade and a now derelict clock tower. Trade fell off, Morrie says, because in a street market: 'People can walk down one side and back up the other, and compare prices, but on a square they walk up and down, get a bit lost, forget what they've seen where, and lose interest.'

One further advantage of the linear format stood out as Harry, Lennie and other committee members strung bunting and banners the length of the street to mark the start of the Shopping Festival and Charity Gala held during the last week in February and the first week of March. It was a time for pulling together, though mostly with an eye to trade. The shops gave prizes for the 'mystery envelope' competition and the bookmaker donated a £100 first prize for the Miss Roman Road competition to be staged at the Traders' Dance. The East London Advertiser put up posters and the one-hundred-and-fiftieth Anniversary banners, and there was to be a night out with the belly-dancer at a local restaurant for the lucky winner of the raffle. But there were snags. First there was a shortage of volunteers to climb the ladders to put up bunting, then some stallholders were muttering about attractions in the market drawing away their trade, and the public health department was none too sure about the hot potato stall.

Then, after heavy rain had brought the low-slung bunting even lower, a huge container truck trying to find the Blackwall Tunnel drove straight down Roman Road, as many still do even on market days, taking with it a whole section of the decorations.

But the celebrations of a hundred and fifty years (more or less) of market activity moved on towards their highpoint on Saturday 1 March, and March came in like a lamb, clear and bright. A three-piece band was pulled up and down the road on one of Brian Baker's trolleys, pounding out old Cockney music-hall favourites, followed by the Finchettes troupe who squeezed between the stalls to perform their majorette routines. In the afternoon the band broke into *I'm Henry the Eighth I am* as boxer Henry Cooper, once a greengrocer himself, made his personal appearance on home territory. Signing autographs as he went on walkabout, 'our 'Enery' took his own crowd with him as he countered cracks about his after-shave, sold balloons on the Youth Club's charity stall, and with a smile turned down an invitation to serve behind the Olds' vegetable stall.

Away from the market, the main attraction of the fortnight was the Traders' Annual Dance at the Poplar Civic Theatre. No one actually showed up in a pearly king outfit, but there was no doubt in anyone's mind that this was an occasion to let your hair down, a traditional East End 'knees up'. Lennie, with cream jacket and microphone, a little more nervous than in action on his stall, compèred the Miss Roman Road competition, while Harry da Costa chaired the panel of judges. The traders and their families shared their evening with the Lady Mayor, a number of councillors and even the market inspectors – often looked on by market traders rather as a motorist regards traffic wardens.

As the evening warmed up and a number of Mother Browns showed everyone how to get their knees up, in the middle of it all in one of his natty suits was Mr Lockwood, doing the Lambeth Walk arm in arm with the rest of them.

The closeness of spirit reflected what Harry da Costa had told us of the traders themselves: 'As far as business is concerned, as a general rule we are at each other's throats. But when business is forgotten, we are the best of friends. The spirit amongst us is terrific. If you're in trouble you've only got to open your mouth and there's half a dozen to help you straightaway, financially as well as any other way. We're friendly, co-operative business men.'

Portland

'Let us hope . . . that your quarries may thrive, that your skills and crafts be exercised.'

On a weekday each November in recent years, Cecil Durston, a retired stonemason known to nearly everyone on Portland as 'Skylark', has put on his best suit and set off for lunch in his local 'castle', Pennsylvania Castle, now a comfortable, privately-owned hotel. Skylark Durston is one of twenty-four 'commoners' of Portland who are summoned each year to the hotel by the Queen's Bailiff to attend the Court Leet of the Island and Royal Manor of Portland. Before lunch the day's business begins as the Deputy Crown Steward swears in the twenty-four jurors: 'You shall diligently inquire and true Presentment make of all such matters and things as you shall be given in charge; the Queen's counsel, your own and your fellows' you shall keep secret; you shall present nothing out of hatred, malice or ill will; you shall not conceal anything out of fear, favour or affection, but in all things you shall well and truly present as the same shall come to your knowledge. So help you God.'

The Court Leet is first recorded around 872 when King Alfred was Lord of the Manor. Edward the Confessor granted Portland to the Monastery of St Swithin at Winchester in 1042, but William the Conqueror reaffirmed it as a Royal Manor in 1078. In 1100 Henry I granted it to the monastery for the second time, but by the end of the fifteenth century the Manor was once again part of Crown lands. Portland has retained its special connection with the Crown ever since.

Portland is still referred to by its inhabitants as an island, though it is in fact a peninsula which has been described as 'a barren lump of rock jutting half-way to France'. This immense block of limestone, four and-a-half miles long and one and-a-half miles wide is joined to the mainland by Chesil Bank, a fourteen-mile-long sweeping rampart of pebbles which is negotiable only with difficulty even on foot. So until Ferry Bridge was built in 1839, Portland was accessible only by

Chesil Bank – fourteen miles of pebbles

boat and remained largely isolated from outside influences. Its inhabitants retained the characteristics of islanders, and customs and practices survived long after they were obsolete elsewhere. Even after the bridge was built, marriage with 'kimberlins' or outsiders, remained a rarity, and still today 'islanders' have a natural reserve with strangers and are fiercely jealous of their independence. As part of local government reorganisation in 1974 Portland and its traditional enemy, the neighbouring town of Weymouth, were amalgamated, but Portland still retains its own Town Council and Mayor. More significant perhaps is the survival of the Court Leet which retains its power to administer the common lands of the island, despite the abolition of most of England's remaining independent courts by the Administration of Justice Act of 1977.

A communal system of agriculture with open fields farmed by freehold tenants survived into the twentieth century, and some strip farming still continues today. This created an obvious need for close

A corner of Portland Harbour: a natural deep-water harbour improved for the
Navy in the nineteenth century

co-operation in farming and, coupled with the gap left by an absent
Lord of the Manor, was enough to ensure the continuing existence of
a strong system of self-government, the manorial court. There is of
course one other outstanding reason why the court has survived and
representatives of the Crown Commissioners have continued to travel
down to Portland once a year to meet the commoners – the world-
famous Portland stone.

Quarrying the 'King of the Oolites' has been the staple industry of
Portland for centuries. It was used on buildings in London as early as
the fourteenth century, but it was first made fashionable in the early-
seventeenth century by Inigo Jones. He used it in the construction of
a number of important buildings including the Banqueting Hall for
the new Whitehall Palace, now thought to be the oldest surviving
building using Portland stone. Until recent years stone has been a

steady source of income for both the Crown and its tenants. By ancient custom the tenants received half the duty paid on stone raised on common land – which at the time of a survey in 1650 was apparently a total of twelve pence per ton. In 1664 Charles II boosted the tenants' share to three-quarters of the duty payable, mainly, it seems, out of gratitude for the loyalty they had shown to their Lord of the Manor, his father, during the Civil War.

Few could have foreseen at that time the great boom in the use of Portland stone which started in the 1670s when Sir Christopher Wren began rebuilding St Paul's Cathedral and the City churches following the Great Fire of 1666. As the demand for Portland stone became more and more widespread, so the revenue which flowed into His Majesty's Stone Grant Fund increased, until by the 1850s it reached the considerable sum of about £200 per annum. Even as recently as the 1930s a total of 100,000 tons of stone was being quarried in Portland annually, although by this time mainly from private land. Then, shortly before the Second World War, a revolution in building methods brought in 'box-building', and later the large-scale use of concrete and reconstituted facing stone resulted in a massive decline in the use of natural block stone. The mini boom of post-war reconstruction too was short-lived.

For some years now the two remaining private quarries have not taken any stone from taxable land, so the Court Leet's funds have been severely depleted. Now its only income derives from such sources as common land let out as public car parks and annually-reviewed rentals or 'fines' for 'encroachments' such as driveways to private houses which must cross 'common' verges to reach the road. But from its remaining funds the Court continues to hand out annually charitable grants to bodies such as churches, scout troops and play groups, as it did in the past to needy individuals in the community. The simple fact of continuity seems to lend an air of optimism to the occasion as Skylark Durston and the assembled jurors, many with family names like Lynham, Pearce, Stone, White and Comben, names recorded at the Court Leet down the centuries, relax with church-warden pipes after lunch. At the end of the morning's formal business the Crown Steward's words had caught the mood: 'It is to be regretted that no stone has been raised since the last Court. Let us hope that the building industry may soon return to use the stone, that your quarries may thrive, that your skills and crafts be exercised and that this country may again have new buildings of the beauty and elegance of Portland stone to add to the nation's heritage.'

On any large scale of course that would seem a vain hope, but with the ever-rising cost of other building materials such as bricks, steel and concrete, there are increasing signs of a return to the use of natural stone in parts of the country where it is readily available, as we discovered in the Cotswolds (see Chapter 12). As if in readiness, a nucleus of workers retain the skills once common to virtually every working man in Portland. There are still two quarries operating, and a few freelance quarrymen. Young Dave Gould has learned from his father, Terry, arts such as 'feathering' – splitting the huge blocks of stone precisely by driving in lines of spikes between steel wedges. Not many years ago every hole in the ground in this pocked, almost treeless landscape would have echoed to the steady rhythm of the hammers, but now very few sons even get the opportunity to pick up the skills of their fathers.

Skylark Durston is a living example of the heights achieved by some of Portland's craftsmen. As a mason though, his skills represent a far newer tradition in Portland than those of the quarrymen. Until the coming of the railways in the nineteenth century, the stone blocks had always been sent away in their raw state to be worked at their final sites by bands of itinerant masons. Sir Christopher Wren had shipped raw stone from seven piers on the east side of the island direct to the banks of the Thames for the construction of St Paul's. But once railways made it possible to transport worked stone with little risk of damage, masonry yards sprang up in Portland alongside the quarries, and the masons flocked in on the promise of a more settled way of life from traditional stone-working areas such as Derbyshire, Yorkshire, Somerset and other parts of Dorset.

The building trade though has always suffered its slumps as well as enjoyed its booms, and life on a relatively barren lump of rock like Portland could obviously be tough in the slack times. Such circumstances bred into the Portlanders their capacity for hard work and their versatility, although they started off with a number of advantages over the inland peasants of Dorset. Not only were stone and driftwood freely available to build comfortable homes, there was also fish from the sea to supplement their agriculture. The Rev. J. Hutchins observed in his famous *History of Dorset* (1774), that the people of

Cecil 'Skylark' Durston

Portland were 'better fed than any I think I have ever seen.'

Today, educational opportunities have broadened the horizons, but when Skylark left school the stone trades were virtually unavoidable for all the young men of Portland. His experience was typical: 'As a boy I just became an apprentice stone mason, which is what I expected. Every boy here expected to go into stone in some way or other, either the quarries or masonry. I went into masonry, and then when the slump came in the thirties I went to London to find work and had several stretches there working on such things as the Barkers of Kensington building and the restoration of the Houses of Parliament. That was between long spells of enforced idleness back at home. Eventually I went fishing for a living for two years off the Bill, but then the man I went fishing with was urged by his family to take on his nephew, so I was given the boot. But before the war broke out, I was back in the stone yard.'

Since the war, Skylark's own particular skills have kept him employed and even now he finds himself quite often recalled from retirement to work again in the very shed where he started his career as one of forty apprentices. There were only two apprentices when we filmed him there in March 1978 working on one of his 'special jobs', assisting sculptor John Main shape up his latest work in Portland stone. Main freely admitted that it would have taken him months to do what Skylark's eye for the stone could achieve in weeks. In 1959 Skylark and his workmates at the Stone Firms Ltd. were approached by another sculptor and asked to carve a set of highly complex figures representing the triumph of light over darkness to decorate the top of the AEI building (now British Steel) in Grosvenor Place, London. He felt he needed the mason, the man who knew the stone, to give the raw material the skill his concept deserved. Unlike their itinerant predecessors, masons like Skylark now have to travel simply to see their work in its final situation. He came with us to London to see the figures on the AEI building for the first time, but afterwards he told us his favourite piece of work was in Cardiff: 'I think every craftsman at some time or other does a job which he is particularly pleased with. If all the Portland stone ever worked could be drawn together in a crown, for me its jewel would be Cardiff City Centre. On seeing it for the first and only time a few years ago, I felt very proud to have been part of it.'

There are very few in the stone sheds today to share that kind of pride, but in his early days the sheds rang to the hammers and songs of the apprentices, which is how young Cecil Durston came by his nickname. On his first day the foreman named him 'Skylark', the most tuneful apprentice! On Portland, nicknames, at one time almost universal, were often humorous in form but usually more serious in purpose. As in other closed communities, intermarriage was common and surnames were relatively few, so with few Christian names in common use, nicknames became a necessity to distinguish between individuals with the same formal names. One may well wonder what personal characteristics typified 'Trot', 'Saltcellar' and 'Bobbycock' Pearce, or a list of Stones that reads like a version of the Seven Dwarfs – 'Nod', 'Row', 'Bowls', 'Bun' and 'Luney'.

Because of the island's almost total isolation until the first bridge was built, marriage between Portlanders was very much the rule. In the first half of the nineteenth century only about one in eighteen of marriages at St George's Church involved an outsider, and furthermore at the vast majority of Portland weddings the bride would be pregnant. Until well into the nineteenth century it was the custom to prove the union fertile before marriage, but once the girl was pregnant, marriage was regarded as automatic. As a result there were very few illegitimate births, but this part of the bargain often caught outsiders by surprise, as the engineer John Smeaton, who built the Eddystone Lighthouse, discovered in 1756 when his guide round the quarries, a Mr Roper, told him:

> On coming down from London, our men were much struck and mighty pleased with the facility of the Portland ladies; and it was not long before several of the women proved with child; but the men being called upon to marry them this part of the lesson they were uninstructed in. On their refusal, the Portland women arose to stone them out of the Isle . . .

This habit of hurling rocks at strangers is the likely origin of the name 'Isle of Slingers' given to Portland by Thomas Hardy in his novel *The Well-beloved*.

The Portland custom that brought about the most tragi-comic results was that of Gavelkind, the system of inheritance applied to the property of those who died intestate until as late as 1926. The property or land went, not to the eldest son alone, but to all sons equally. The ensuing complications of ownership, where a man might own an eighth part of a quarter share in a piece of land or property, made the exact marking out and division of the 'lynchets' or strips of farming land essential, and evidence of the balks, or unploughed strips, between them can still be seen.

The fate of the beautiful St George's Church in the middle of the island illustrates the most lunatic results of the Gavelkind tradition. The building still stands against the crisp light of the island like an implant from the Mediterranean, still surrounded by some of the oldest graves in Portland repetitiously recording the old family names, but it has no congregation! Not surprisingly, St George's bears a resemblance to Wren's city churches since it was built in the mid-eighteenth century by Thomas Gilbert, whose forebear and namesake had at one time been Wren's agent in Portland. St George's was built to replace St Andrew's which had been costing a fortune in repairs as it quietly slipped down the cliffs of Church Ope Cove over the years, and which had become too small for a population expanded by the stone industry. Various means were used to raise the money for St George's, including payments from the Stone Grant Fund, an appeal to King George II, a parish levy and finally the outright sale of pews to residents. After several generations and the effects of Gavel-kind, the ownership of these pews became so complicated that half the congregation finished up outside the church, while inside half the pews stood empty. By the early years of the twentieth century when modernisation was proposed the problems of establishing ownership proved so complex that finally it was decided to abandon St George's and build a new church, All Saints, which was consecrated in 1917. Thanks to the Friends of St George's and the Redundant Churches Fund, St George's has survived as a remarkable, unaltered example of an eighteenth-century church interior.

In Portland there are much more vivid memories of less godly pastimes than churchgoing. Smuggling and wrecking were almost universal pursuits, and continued well within living memory. The hidden bay of Church Ope Cove was a favourite run ashore for smugglers, while on the west side of the island the locals kept watch on stormy nights along the shifting pebbles of Chesil Beach for the inevitable wrecks. Tales are told here as elsewhere about lanterns tied to cows' tails to mislead unwary sailors, and here as elsewhere are equally likely to be untrue. Given a south-westerly gale blowing into Deadman's Bay, as it was known in Hardy's day, such devices were hardly necessary. If a sailing vessel failed to stand off far enough to round the Bill, itself a hazardous exercise because of the Portland Race, a turbulent stretch of water half-a-mile to the south, it would be blown relentlessly up into the bay and thrown on to Chesil Beach by the breakers.

Only the Portland 'lerret', a specially-developed type of fishing craft, could be expected to land in reasonable safety on these shifting stones and then only in the calmest of weather. The 'lerret', developed from Norwegian surf boats and tapered to stem and stern from a broad beam, put to sea with the aid of a shore crew and landed backwards with the six- or eight-man crew pushing on the oars. The object was to ride the crest of a wave and land as high on the beach as possible to avoid being dragged back by the next breaker and its undertow full of rolling pebbles.

Portlanders and their lerrets had their heroic moments, as on the stormy morning of 12 September 1877 when a boatload of twelve survivors of the sailing-ship *Forest* were seen heading for the shore. In a force-eight gale the night before, the *Forest* and the emigrant ship *Avalanche* had collided twelve miles south-west of Portland Bill, and now the only survivors were in danger of being swept to their deaths on the beach. Fourteen Portlanders in two lerrets put out to the boat, transferred the exhausted survivors and brought them safely to shore. The fishermen were each rewarded with £9 7s 4d from a public collection and later relatives and friends of those lost aboard the *Avalanche* began a fund which resulted in the building of the Avalanche Memorial Church in the village of Southwell.

On the debit side it can be assumed that, since the law forbade the taking of property from the survivors of shipwreck, on some earlier occasions a few unfortunate sailors may have met their end other than by drowning, but for the most part the Portlanders' involvement in wrecking consisted of the simple assumption that whatever blew ashore was common property. On one notable night in January 1748 after the wreck of a Dutch treasure ship the *Hope* the beach was reportedly thronged for days with crowds of up to four thousand who took away over £25,000 worth of valuables, mainly in gold. At the subsequent trial of a token Portlander, Augustin Elliot, all the evidence from witnesses on shore, including one John Komben, openly supported Elliott, and he was found not guilty.

It needs little imagination, sitting in the bar of the Cove House Inn on Chesil Beach as the powerful swell sucks at the shingle, to picture those days as seventy-year-old Tim Comben, undoubted descendant of John Komben, sups his pint and relates his own impulses to those of his notorious ancestors: 'One Comben was a lighthouse keeper in 1717 at the old lighthouse on Portland Bill. And I suppose all of us could let out a bit of roguery now and then if it was beneficial to anybody. I'd do anything myself if I had to, if I was starving wouldn't you? I wouldn't worry about the law. If I was starving and I saw anything I wanted, I'd have it. You got to exist, ain't you? Especially in those days when the poor devils had no dole.'

Tim now supplements his living as a pensioner by making fishing rods from driftwood and shell dolls for the families of visitors, referred to locally as 'grockles', but his eyes have a glow when he speaks of the old days and the rogues he knew: 'There was Elliot, Tar Elliott and them – when a ship used to hit the beach or the rocks they thought they owned her! Then Levi Green stepped in and he was just as bad – a bigger rogue never walked.' The crowd in the pub laugh, thinking he is a bit carried away by his 'Long John Silver' routine, but Tim is determined to have us believe him: ''Tis right enough! I knew him all me life. And the last time I seen Tar Elliott – John his real name was – I said, "How many sovereigns you got left, John?" and he said, "Enough to make two curled-handled walking-sticks!" And I'm telling you,' said Tim, curling a finger in the air, 'there's thirteen golden sovereigns to an inch. Did you know that?'

The pub is a natural setting for a yarner like Tim who uses the occasion of talking to us to deplore the disappearance of other aspects of the Portland social scene: 'I was a quarryman myself and I worked with the Spitfly gang, a fishermen's gang. I recall us being on the booze three days at a time, and I'm not ashamed of it. There was "Bootstrings", "Pigtails", my brother Norman, Roscoe Board, Teddy Board, me, and Alec Gould. We'd work up till Wednesday, then we'd shout up to the crane driver, "Put your derrick down, Dick", and that was it; we'd be in the New Inn till Saturday. I'm not ashamed of it. I'd do it again if I had the chance. But I'm a bloody old age pensioner now and you can't do it. Anyway, things have changed. When I was working up that quarry, there were six hundred and eighty quarrymen and three men done the books for the lot. Now they've got four hundred and fifty people doing the books and four quarrymen!'

Again the customers in the Cove House roar with laughter, but this time the joke is nearer to the bone. Both the quarry where Tim worked and the stoneyard where Skylark was apprenticed as a stone-mason are now run by subsidiaries of the Bath and Portland Stone Company with headquarters in the West Country. For many old Portlanders like Tim, to see the remnants of their declining stone industry run almost exclusively by outsiders is to feel an increasing sense of remoteness from the trade that has provided most Portlanders' bread and butter for centuries. 'Portland has lost its birthright,' Tim said. 'It'd pay them better to put a bloody iron gate across Weymouth Road and keep the strangers out.' A traditional Portland sentiment!

For all an old man's passion for a return to the 'good old days', Portland's salvation in the face of a fluctuating stone trade has always been the adaptability and ingenuity of the Portlanders themselves. So, as in other places we have visited, the onus has been on the sons to adapt, innovate or leave. Tim Comben's forty-year-old son John has tried all three and is still open-minded about the future. 1978 found him back home in Portland in successful pursuit of the latest in-

John Comben, trained a stonemason, has tried his hand at many jobs. Now he
is fishing for spider crabs

novation – selling spider crabs to the Spaniards. Every week or two in
the season, he and his partner Brian 'Fishy' Newton were conducting
thousands of pounds' worth of business in the bar of a dockside pub
with the driver of a huge refrigerated Spanish lorry. John sat on the
dockside while he waited to load the live crabs into the lorry's salt-
water tanks, and recalled the twists of fortune that seemed to have
determined his own career: 'When I left school there wasn't really a
lot of choice – be a quarryman, or a stonemason, or move away. I
started as a stonemason because I was very interested in the job, but
the firm I was working for went more into the square block type

Spider crabs being unloaded on Portland. Most are exported to Spain

building. The craftsmanship part of it seemed to be dying away, so I got out and went fishing.' In the next few years he tried crane driving, a job as a ship's mechanic, drilling and pile-driving, and fishing out of Plymouth and the Channel Islands. Eventually he went back to masonry and decided to try his luck in Australia where he found a big demand for stonemasons to work on the restoration of public buildings.

Then came the unexpected call back to Portland: 'Brian had picked up this idea of selling spider crabs to the Spaniards. He was dealing with a Spanish chap in London and flying them out in boxes from Heathrow. It got too big for him to handle so he dropped me a line. Brian and I had always done a bit of fishing together since we left school, so I didn't hesitate.'

Spider crabs were considered a menace in the past. They got in the pots and kept the lobsters and red crabs out, and since only the locals seemed to want to eat them most fishermen smashed them on the gunwhale, and threw them back. That was soon changed by John and Brian's little enterprise: 'It's certainly doubled the local fisherman's outlook on life. Before, their trade was just a few crabs locally, and a few to the buyers who used to send them up to London, but now everything you can get will go to Spain.'

As we filmed in March 1978, some doubt hung over the future of the spider crab bonanza. The lorries travelled overland through France and were having trouble with EEC regulations, but John Comben remained philosophical: 'I think that given a chance, most of us round here are pretty adaptable. Most of the young chaps I know have played around with a bit of fishing, and it's always there if you want to drop into it, you know. Like a lot of other things. But if the spider crabs go down the Swanee, I'd go back to Australia, be a stonemason again or try the fishing out there. If you're prepared to do anything, you'll get a job. If you fail, they can only sack you, they can't lock you up can they?'

That joke too is double-edged in Portland whose complement of 'outsiders' includes the inmates of both a prison and a Borstal. The eastern side of the island is dominated by the grey towers of the old prison, now the Borstal, which was built in the 1850s, its grim outline reminiscent of Dartmoor. The style of the period is instantly recognisable. Many men before John Comben left Portland for Australia, though unwillingly, for Portland Prison represented an experimental step forward in the penal system, where prisoners sentenced to transportation could earn, by public works and good behaviour, more lenient treatment once they were shipped to the colonies. The main object in building the prison, though, was the public works, part of a cunning economic system – plant a penal colony, get the convicts to hew stone from the quarry next door, and then use their muscle to build the Portland Breakwater. In the days of sail the Portland Roads were the only reasonably secure anchorage between Plymouth and Portsmouth, and a breakwater had long been planned to increase its size and safety. Work on the breakwater continued until 1872, by which time the highest point of the island, commanding the harbour and its entrances, had also been converted by the convicts into the Verne citadel, a vast military fortress which outlived its usefulness in the twentieth century and became the island's prison. The breakwaters, further improved and added to since 1872, continue to provide a deep-water harbour of over four square miles. It was from Portland Roads that American troops left for the invasion of Normandy in 1944, and the harbour is still of considerable strategic importance to the Navy.

The naval base is also of considerable importance to Portland since, with the decline of the stone industry, the Navy has long been the island's biggest employer. In the days of the Spanish Armada it was mainly Dorset lads who sailed out of Portland, but now warships and seamen of many nations come here to the sea training base to be put through their paces by the Royal Navy. We filmed one of their training exercises, a simulated air and missile attack on a flotilla which included a West German destroyer, an attack made all the more testing for those concerned by being staged in one of the roughest bits of sea in the world, the Portland Race, in a force-eight gale! On board HMS *Birmingham*, we talked to Chris Seal, Commander, Sea Training, about his personal experience of contacts with the Portlanders: 'When I was a cadet at Dartmouth my first run ashore was from a frigate here. I've always thought the Navy and the Portlanders have very friendly relationships. There's a tradition of good seafaring chaps from here, they understand what we're trying to do here, and of course the Naval Base provides a lot of local jobs.'

From the rating's point of view a run ashore need not take him very far. Within a hundred yards of the dock gates is a row of five pubs that cater for most of their needs. Inside one of them we asked a bunch of young sailors how they felt they got on with the Portlanders. Most said that getting their 'wets' [drinks] meant little involvement with the locals, but one Yorkshire seaman had weighed up the situation: 'When Jack [a sailor] gets a run ashore here, he's generally on the bimble [a night out] right? Well, if you take the Navy away, Portland itself is nothing, and these pubs wouldn't be able to run. It's only the Navy that keeps these pubs going, the same as the jobs in the dockyard. Close down the Navy connection and there's a lot of Portland people got no work.'

Strong words from an outsider, but many Portland people recognise the truth in them. There is little open resentment against the Navy in Portland, in fact anything that brings in money, be it spider crabs or Jolly Jack, will at the very least be tolerated. At the same time in some quarters positive steps are being taken to preserve what heritage there is for the next generation. Portland children still play a form of hopscotch on a pitch marked out like an ammonite, the stone fossil that is the island's emblem, and there are those who feel that small differences such as these represent more than just a folksy charm. When a few years ago, Dorset County Council was considering a scheme to bus hundreds of Portland schoolchildren to Weymouth, a group led by John Neimer, who married into a Portland family, lobbied fervently against the proposals. Mr Neimer said they felt that children were very much a part of the community: 'Without them the community is losing a great deal in its everyday life and in its future. If children are taken out of their own environment to school, where they are not influenced by the day to day things of our life here, then this will detract from the community in the future.' Such feelings helped the campaign to a successful conclusion and for the moment at least Portland children under sixteen continue to receive their education on the island.

Skylark Durston, no romantic himself, insists on being optimistic about the future of Portland as a community, although his philosophy contains a degree of compromise over old Portland attitudes to 'kimberlins': 'It's difficult for the new people to get to know the old, and it's difficult for the Portland people to communicate with the new. But eventually I think it will be put right by the next generation. The children of newcomers will go to school with Portland children and this, I think, will close the gap. It's bound to change the character of the island eventually, but we shall become a community again.'

St Just-in-Penwith

'The Cornishman is an individual, not given to collective action.'

The landscape between St Ives and Land's End is familiar to many people as the backdrop to the *Poldark* and *Penmarric* television series, a place where dramatic cliffs dip down to the swell of the Atlantic and where once apparently equally dramatic gentry paraded their lives and loves. Certainly the area has its big houses, though they are mostly tucked away out of the wind behind the Cornish 'hedges', the stone and turf embankments that divide the patchwork of tiny fields. Much more dominant in this windswept, almost treeless landscape are the clean-cut stone skeletons of tin-mine engine houses along the coastline and the rows of tin-miners' cottages in St Just and Pendeen and in the smaller communities of Botallack, Carnyorth and Trewellard, Kelynack and Tregeseal, all of which go to make up the parish of St Just-in-Penwith.

The people are warm and hospitable, which often enough the landscape is not. Gales blow in from the Atlantic and sea mists hang over the cliffs, and even on warm summer days the temperature will be a few degrees lower than in the almost Mediterranean atmosphere of palm-fringed Penzance, or the familiar tourist-traps of Newlyn and Mousehole, only a few miles to the east.

The litter of mine workings across the area is a testimony to the generations of miners who have eked a living out of the tin in this granite outcrop since at least the early eighteenth century. It was dramatic falls in the price of tin, especially in the 1860s, as larger and more easily worked deposits were opened up around the world, and again in the 1930s, that laid waste the majority of these independent enterprises, both here and in Cornwall's bigger tin-mining area of Camborne and Redruth.

Miners left in their thousands to seek their fortunes in the new fields of hard-rock mining in Africa, Australia and the Americas. Many of the grey gravestones in Pendeen churchyard indicate that at least one family member 'died in South Africa', for example. A local

The engine shaft at Crown Mines, Botallack, *c.* 1870

saying still has it that 'where a hole is sunk in the ground, no matter in what corner of the globe, you'll be sure to find a Cornishman at the bottom of it, searching for metal'.

These are the 'Cousin Jacks', the expatriates from West Cornwall who have traditionally looked west to the New World before they looked east to the rest of England, or even Cornwall. Questioned some years ago in the radio programme, *Down Your Way*, an old St Just man revealed he had never been east of Hayle, where the Penwith peninsula joins the rest of Cornwall. But the purpose of his various visits there had been to take ship to many other parts of the world. No Cornishman, they will tell you, has ever made a fortune out of Cornish tin, but with the price of tin climbing to well over £8000 a ton in 1980, the industry has rallied. The process of extracting the tin oxide from the ore is difficult and complex – 'there are no bonanzas in tin' is an expression we heard more than once – but higher prices and a reasonably stable market have made new investment in the few surviving companies possible. Among these companies one of the healthiest is Geevor Mine at Pendeen, where well over one million pounds has been invested in development in three years.

Although Geevor Mine is vital to the community as its major employer and, as one local councillor put it, 'they keep the place solvent by paying their rates promptly', both agriculture and, though less obviously, tourism, are probably bigger money makers for the area itself. The soil is not particularly fertile, but because the climate is mild and practically frost-free all the year round, the farmers specialise in market gardening, growing crops such as early potatoes and broccoli, as well as keeping dairy herds and rearing beef cattle. Tourism too is increasing.

Although there are still not many tourist coaches parked in the car park off the square in St Just, more motorists every year clog the scenic coastal road from St Ives to Land's End, stop off at the cottages advertising 'Bed and Breakfast' or call in at Geevor Mine's recently-opened museum to take a guided tour round the surface workings.

The deeper workings and vigorous life of the community itself are altogether too private a world for the casual visitor to penetrate. The area has an atmosphere referred to kindly enough by young Cornishmen further east as 'antique Cornwall', if only because of a quiet determination here to preserve that curious mixture of romanticism and simple practicality, folk wisdom and Christian nonconformity that is the essence of life on the 'Celtic fringe'.

Interest in the Old Cornwall Society and its activities has been growing in recent years, as in other parts of Cornwall, but perhaps symbolic of its strength in West Penwith is the crowd which gathers on Chapel Carn Brea, two miles south of St Just and seven hundred feet above sea level, for the Midsummer Bonfire. The lighting of this bonfire at sunset on Midsummer Eve is the signal for the start of a chain of bonfires from here to the Devon border. The ceremony was restored in 1929, but has its origins in remote pagan times and almost certainly derives from sun worship. As the sun sinks beyond Land's End, the Master of Ceremonies steps forward and says in Cornish: '*Tan yn cynys, Lemmyn gor uskys*' (Now set the pyre, At once on fire), and after the fire is lit, the Lady of the Flowers casts bunches of symbolic herbs into the flames.

The *Plen-an-Gwary*, or 'playing place', in the centre of St Just is one of only two medieval amphitheatres left in England, both of them

Cornish wrestling in the St Just *Plen-an-Gwary*. Observers with sticks are the adjudicators, known as 'sticklers'.

in Cornwall. It is the scene, in summer, of occasional re-enactments of ancient local Mystery plays, and of Cornish wrestling, conducted in thick canvas jackets in the same style as wrestling across the Channel in Celtic Brittany. St Just Feast, too, originally held in July to celebrate the dedication of the Parish Church in 1336, but moved to the Sunday nearest All Saints' Day, 1 November, is still a weekend of some celebration, though nowadays without the great miners' rock-drilling contests and the wild drinking that survived into the present century.

John Wesley, who visited St Just ten times altogether, wrote in 1744:

> It is remarkable that those of St Just were the chief of the whole country for hurling, fighting, drinking and all manner of wickedness, but many of the lions are becoming lambs, and are continually praising God and calling their companions in sin to come and magnify the Lord together.

The tradition of nonconformity that Wesley began in Cornwall is still in evidence, though those who are intent on the revival of Cornish, which died out as a spoken language at the end of the eighteenth century, will remind you that Wesley was apparently one of those who opposed its continued use. The revival of interest in Cornish identity has taken hold particularly in communities like St Just and finds expression in organisations like Mebyon Kernow (Sons of Cornwall), principally a cultural movement, but now with strong political ambitions. Apart from a few local councillors, its success at the polls is small, though there is widespread approval for many of its ideals. As Hugh Miners, deputy Grand Bard of the Cornish Gorsedd who lives in St Just, explained: 'The Cornishman is an individual, not given to collective action.' The Cornish identity, even as far as fellow-Cornishmen are concerned, remains a very personal matter.

Since childhood, Laura Rowe has been expressing her joy and pride in her Cornish heritage by painting and drawing, and anyone walking the breath-taking cliff-tops at Botallack or Cape Cornwall should not be surprised to come across this small, bright-eyed lady with her sketch-pad. Both she and her husband John, now retired from his job as a miner at Geevor, come from local families with strong mining traditions, although Laura's father also did the usual bit of farming: 'Most people in the mines had their smallholdings as well. Father worked at Wheal Cock and had a smallholding, and he kept sheep on the cliff in between. Each morning when he went to work, he'd tend to his sheep and on his way back he'd look to them again. His father had a small farm with pigs and dairy as well, but when they sank the new shaft, they covered his potato field with spoil from the mine.'

John Rowe's father was one of the Cousin Jacks who went to South Africa, where he was well-known as a wrestling champion, until, after working at home again and another spell in South Africa, he died at the early age of forty-eight. Before the days of wet-drilling and face masks, silicosis claimed many lives in middle-age or earlier, through the miners' breathing in the glass-sharp granite dust. In the 1930s many young men were frightened off by the 'dust deaths' of their fathers, but young John Rowe followed in his father's footsteps to South Africa. After he had been out there for nearly ten years, he came home for a holiday and met Laura. They were married in 1945, and since there was now work in the mines, he decided to stay in Cornwall.

Cornish tin miners in 1919. This group worked on the development of the
Wheal Carne mine

John was obviously lucky in more ways than one, and both he and
Laura still count themselves fortunate to be established in their own
part of Cornwall. Even since 1945 many young people have had to
go away to find work and wealthier outsiders have bought up the
cottages, often as 'second-homes'. Both Laura and John are members of Mebyon Kernow, but Laura insists that her interest is not
really political: 'I think it's just a defensive thing. Before, our friends
were all around us, but now that we're scattered our sense of being
Cornish has drawn us together. We want to protect and conserve the
place, the people and its ways – the old ways. It's the honesty I want
to keep. The thing is, we've got all these societies, the Council for the
Preservation of Rural England and all these people, they're marvel-
lous people, but they've got no teeth. *We're* losing something valuable
and *they* can't do anything about it. The exploiters have got the top
say all the time.'

Laura's compulsion to draw and paint the local landscape has a
touch of romance perhaps, but is a feeling obviously shared by the

Edward Waters near his home

many local people in whose homes her work hangs: 'I have a very
protective instinct, and that's what makes me draw the plants and
small animals. Drawing the old crosses and churches is a conservation
thing to me. When I walk around this narrow peninsula, I feel the
things I heard about as a child. I know the miners used to play pitch
and toss, and if you're sitting in the old pitch and toss ground, it's
nice, it's homely. It's not sinister to us at all. Your feet are somewhere
in the ground, and it's necessary for me, at my age, to feel like that.'

It would be quite wrong to give the impression that all visitors are
unwelcome. The people of Penwith can be almost overwhelmingly
hospitable, and anyone who takes the trouble to pass the time of day
and show an interest in the people and their environment stands to be
treated kindly. Perhaps there will first be objections to the influx of
'second-homers', well-off retired people, and caravanners who bring
little to the community but congested roads, but most local people
accept that visitors who stay in the area bring some advantages
through the small businesses and service industries that rely on their

trade. But having set these topics aside, the Cornishman, like all good Celts, enjoys good conversation and the opportunity to tell a tale or two.

In Carnyorth, a mile or so nearer the mine than the Rowes' cottage, Edward and Ivy Waters open up their home each summer to bed and breakfast guests. Edward's pleasure in recounting mining stories made him an obvious choice to show visitors round the Geevor Museum when a back injury put a stop to his life underground a few years ago, a life he had chosen with some determination: 'I was only a few months old when my father, who had been a miner, was killed in France in the First War. My mother was only a young woman, so I was brought up by my grandparents and my great-uncles. All my family were in mining, and I began at Geevor mine at the age of fourteen in 1930. But when I was sixteen in order to keep my father's war pension until I was twenty-one, I had to go for an apprenticeship. So I took up carpentering, but my mind was really down there, underground. My grandma didn't want me to go down, but after war broke out and I'd served with the Royal Engineers in bomb disposal, thirty-five of us got called back from service. In the meantime my grandma had died, so I was all right. I went down. At first I did mining in general. I had a go at everything down there, and finished up as shaftmaster. One day one of the managers said to me, "Edward, you're like a clown in a circus". I said that wasn't a very nice thing to say, and asked him what he meant. He said, "A clown's the smartest man in the circus, and that's like you here. We can put you to any job underground, and you'll go and do it." Every time there was an accident and I was called out, Ivy got more and more upset and tried to persuade me to come up to the surface, but I told her, "Underground's my life, and I want to stop down there". Well, in 1974 I had an accident myself. A pipe was dropped in the shaft and it came down and caught me in the spine, and after I'd been at home two years with that, the doctor said, "You're not going back in that mine no more."'

Ivy's fears about the mine had taken root at an early age. Her father had died of silicosis at the age of thirty-eight leaving five children of which she was the youngest. Then her husband was not to be persuaded to take a surface job, and their two sons, Eugene and Nigel, as they grew up, became in their father's own words 'mine-mad'. But because of her fears, both sons promised their mother that they would never go down the mine while she was alive. Nigel now works in the mine sawmill, and Eugene, the older brother, went away to the RAF. Edward clearly understands their feelings about working underground, but is proud that they have kept their word.

For visitors to the mine museum Edward's stories emphasise the spirit of adventure as much as the hardships: 'I tell them that up to 1830 there were well over three hundred mines working in Cornwall, employing twenty-one thousand miners, and five to six thousand women and boys over the age of eight. But when alluvial deposits were found in places like Malaya, Cornish mining became too expensive and many had to leave, starting in the 1830s. Many of the Cousin Jacks went due west to New York, and on to open up the mines in Michigan. You'll see their graves in Michigan, Montana, Arizona, Pennsylvania, Colorado, and right down in California. I've got cousins down there in California.'

Perhaps it is only natural, when speaking of your own community, to omit the worst of the statistics. In 1850 the average age of death in St Just was twenty seven, and the causes were as much poverty and malnutrition as silicosis and tuberculosis. In the 1870s St Just's population fell from nine thousand to little over six thousand and altogether one third of Cornwall's mining population left the county – the less adventurous of them perhaps turning up to dig the docks in Hull or open up the coal-mines in Northumberland, as we have seen in previous chapters.

Edward himself was tempted to try his luck in South Africa when his children were young, but eventually decided against it. Instead, he and Ivy have broadened their base by taking in visitors, and Edward's yarns of the miners form part of the entertainment. Edward and Ivy have the Cornishman's natural delight in welcoming visitors, but they would like to see controls on visitors who come back to buy up houses: 'These second houses shut up in the winter-time mean young Cornish couples shut out. I think the councils should tell people it's all right to come down and buy a house, but you've got to live in it. You can't have it as a second home, or we'll rate you so high that it won't be worthwhile to keep the house.'

Edward's thoughts turned back to mining, and future prospects in that direction: 'I think the tourists do help us, but I would like to see the Government open up some of these mines, especially the coastal mines. In the old days they had to rely on natural ventilation through two shafts, downcast and upcast, but now we've got compressed air extractor fans, we can go much further. So that's where the future of mining is going to be – under the sea.'

One of the most dramatic developments taking place in Cornish tin mining has already moved in this direction, the opening up by Geevor Tin Mines Ltd of the old Levant Mine, closed since 1930 and scene of one of tin mining's worst disasters in 1919. The project has been under serious consideration since the late 1950s, and in 1959 Edward Waters was instrumental in proving that the sea had broken into the old workings. After some set-backs the breach to the sea was finally sealed with a concrete plug in 1965, and in 1979, owing to increased confidence in the industry, work began on a new sub-incline shaft. This will give direct access to the seaward extensions of Geevor's own tin-bearing lodes and the lower workings of the old Levant Mine. In 1980, after months of pumping, short connecting tunnels were driven through and these workings re-entered. The investment has been considerable and hopes are high in the whole community, but even with modern geological techniques, tin-mining is still a risky undertaking.

Even as far back as 1887 the Levant's workings under the sea stimulated the visitor's interest, as can be seen from the account of Frank Ernest Allum who worked for the Royal Mint and was on a walking tour of Cornwall:

In this mine, as in most Cornish mines, the method of descending is by ladders and not, in coal mine fashion, by means of a cage. A candle embedded in a piece of clay was stuck in my hat, and, my guide going first, we commenced our descent. After about eight minutes I asked if we were nearing the bottom. My ideas of depth seemed to amuse my guide somewhat, and he told me I was then at the 160 yards level, and that the bottom was 640 yards . . . [When we reached the 480 yards level my companion said] that I should see nothing different if I went lower down and would have more 'travelling' [climbing] to do on coming up . . . and so it happened that the 480 yards level was the deepest part I reached.

Leaving the bottom of the shaft, we began our subterranean and submarine wanderings . . . It seemed hard to believe that all this was right under the sea, and I thought how little people in the ships going over our heads knew that there were men, and even a steam engine, far down in the earth beneath them.

Frank Allum noted the heat, the constantly-working water pumps, and especially the red, clay-like mud which stained every piece of clothing the miners wore, and even the men themselves. Now he understood why he had been given a complete change of clothes before he entered the mine, as every visitor still is today. He was particularly impressed by the hard slog that was the miner's everyday round once he had reached his place of work:

> The miner takes in his left hand a boring tool, something like a crow-bar which has a chisel-shaped end, and hammers it against the rock. Each time he strikes the head of the tool he turns it round a little, and thus slowly, makes a hole in the rock. The depth to which the holes are made depends upon the thickness of the lode, and the consequent amount of rock it is desirable to dislodge, but the usual depth is about two or three feet. To make one of these holes will take a man a day and half or two days' continued hammering. When the required depth is arrived at, a charge of dynamite is pushed down to the end of the hole, and is fired off by means of a fuse, and a large piece of rock is thus torn away.

He found 'travelling' up the vertical ladders more difficult than the descent, and after eighty fathoms persuaded his guide that they should travel on the 'man-engine'.

> Tom was a little dubious about my venturing on such a machine . . . It consists of a long rod or column, made of baulks of timber about 18 inches by 24 inches in section, which stands in a slightly slanting shaft. On this rod steps are fixed at distances of four fathoms apart with a handle just above them for a man to take hold of. There are stagings built in the shaft at corresponding distances of four fathoms with a hole in each sufficiently large to admit the step to pass through. The rod continually goes up and down a distance of four fathoms. Consequently anyone who wishes to ascend has merely to wait until a step comes down to the staging upon which he stands, and promptly get on it. It will immediately go upwards, carrying him with it. On arriving at the next staging he must step off at once and wait for the next higher step to come down for him, on to this he must get as before, and so on, until he reaches the top.
>
> The use of this 'engine' is not altogether unattended with danger. It is a 'man-engine' in more than one sense. It takes its tribute of a man occasionally. I had not realised that there was much danger, until at one time, when my candle was rather low and consequently I could not

see very well, I put out my foot to get upon the staging just a moment before we were level with it. Fortunately for me my boots were somewhat roomy and my foot did not quite reach the end of this one, which was caught by the staging and suddenly bent down, and my foot itself somewhat hurt by the process. The step did not fit the man-hole very exactly and so I escaped unhurt from what might have been a serious accident.

Thirty-two years later in 1919 a steel strap at the end of the giant rocking beam that operated the man-engine snapped, plunging the column and the men on it to the bottom of the shaft. Thirty-one miners were killed and many more injured. The effect of such an accident on a small community can scarcely be imagined, but to make matters worse, the company could not afford to replace the man-engine with anything safer. The men were told that if the mine were to stay open they would have to walk to work. So then the men of Levant, after walking anything up to five miles on the surface to the mine, climbed down the quarter of a mile of ladders (the lowest levels were abandoned) and walked perhaps another three miles under-ground, before beginning their day's work. The homeward journey no doubt seemed a good deal longer. This continued until the mine finally closed in 1930.

Life around the mines in Pendeen was until recently a bleak existence. Clifford Tresize, who has worked as a maintenance en-gineer at Geevor for thirty years, still lives in the middle of Pendeen. He well remembers his father's little business as a social centre of the village: 'My father had a shoemaker's shop in the village and myself and my three brothers would take jugs of tea up there to him. In between shifts the miners would come in to get their boots mended. In there they would pick the football team, the cricket team, and talk of wrestling and greyhound racing. We were poor, but everybody mucked in. I had to change out of my decent clothes after school, but some children were so poor they had to put cardboard in the soles of their boots when they wore through. Everybody kept geese and fowls, and it would be one of them we'd have for Christmas dinner.'

When Clifford was a boy, complaints about the miners' conditions were beginning to be heard, but it was a lean time for the industry, and many felt they could not afford to lose their jobs, at almost any price: 'I remember about 1930 some of the men had to pay back some of their wages to keep the mine open. And you still used to see houses with wire-mesh instead of glass in the bedroom windows, so that miners with silicosis could breathe at night. If they died of coughing – had a heart attack – that's what it was said they died of, not silicosis, so the families got no compensation. It was still a dusty job, because they didn't start using water until the late thirties. The wages were not really big enough to afford drink, but I reckon they did drink more than they do today. But even now you won't find a rich Cornish miner who made his money here. I can't name anyone with a big house and a big car who got them from Cornish mining.'

Few young Cornishmen today go into the mines, either at home or abroad, but generations of feeling exploited seem to have bred a despair in many young people of ever finding work and fulfilment on their home territory. Clifford Tresize said: 'The Cornishman is his own worst enemy – he sits back while outsiders take over,' and often there does seem to be a lack of drive towards self-help. Enterprise, when it happens, tends to be individual and relatively short-term, rather than far-sighted and collective. Some blame attitudes in local government, and complain that far too many councillors are incomers, while admitting reluctantly that this is largely due to a lack of Cornish candidates, or support for them when they stand. It is true that few home-based Cornishmen have ever had the resources to compete on equal terms with wealthy businessmen from 'up country', but even on a smaller scale there seems a general reluctance to take a gamble with businesses, shops or hotels and play the 'exploiters' at their own game.

Laura Rowe has her own theory: 'I don't think Cornishmen like to be in debt to anybody. They want to be solvent, and that's where they fall down, because other people live on tick. They come down here and swipe everything away from us. It's partly to do with the old religious tradition – absolute scrupulous honesty and not being able to see anything beyond being completely solvent. Most people down here are very honest, very straight. They feel guilty about getting anything on hire purchase – I do myself, I wouldn't dream of it. I'd be scared to, because it wouldn't belong to me at all. I know it's silly but I think a lot of Cornish people are like that. But people from elsewhere make more money and they don't mind borrowing, because that's the way everybody lives now. I think perhaps our younger ones would be more sensible about it.'

The younger element still retains enough of these attitudes to mark them as the children of their parents, but many of the younger members of Mebyon Kernow that we met berate their own parents for leaving them to discover for themselves any real meaning in their Cornish identity. In many cases it was a subject rarely discussed at home, let alone shouted from the rooftops. Even within these groups there were those who had doubts about their long-term effectiveness, and views varied on such subjects as the degree of Cornish self-determination, or even separatism, that they sought. But the principles behind these vocal individuals were summarised by Malcolm Williams, their twenty-six-year-old St Just councillor, as a renewed determination 'to stop the Cornish becoming a minority in their own land'.

Jeremy Green is one of the younger generation who has successfully established himself in his own land. He has been recently appointed a mine captain at Geevor at the age of thirty-one. He now lives in a comfortable converted stone store-house next to the mine museum, where his wife Helen runs the visitors' snack bar. His mother was a Trembath, a well-known name in mining, and his very local roots give him a good deal of sympathy with the Mebyon Kernow line: 'When I was at college, I was never English, I was Cornish, and we made a big thing of being Cornish. In fact I'd go as far as saying that England begins at Hayle. I'm not that keen on second homes either. We've been trying for about five or six years to get a house, and we don't really want to live on one of the new estates. When you haven't got quite enough money for a deposit, you begin to realise that half the homes aren't being built for locals anyway. Then you wonder if *any* of them are for locals, because the locals can't afford to buy them. And it gets to be not just a nuisance, but a pain in the neck. You get the feeling the place is being taken over, especially in the middle of August when it's overrun.'

Jeremy's connection with Geevor goes back to 1967 when he did a three-month stint in the office during vacation from London University. After concentrating on geography at school, he soon specialised in geology at university, and followed that with a year's research at the Camborne School of Mines, all the time filling in his vacations with spells at the mine. After experience of various jobs in the mine, in 1972 he was made one of eight shift-bosses, each in charge of a section of the mine, and in 1976 Mr Gilbert, Geevor's manager, agreed to send him back to Camborne on a full-time basis

Jeremy Green, one of two mine-captains at Geevor

for three years as the mine's sponsored student. He carried off all the prizes, and soon after his return had a chance to broaden his experience as a Cousin Jack, though on a very temporary basis: 'When we left college, we all had to go and work in a mine, and ninety-nine per cent of the other students didn't have a mine to go to. Well, I had Geevor, but I thought it might be more benefit to Geevor if I went to another mine. So I went to see Mr Gilbert and said, "Where do you want me to go?" and he said, "Tasmania". It was another tin mine, but as far as the actual mining is concerned, totally different from Geevor. They just drove huge trucks in there, down an incline.'

Obviously further promotion, perhaps to mine superintendant, is in the air for Jeremy in the next few years, but first he must acquire more experience at Geevor, particular experience that cannot be acquired by a short trip to Tasmania, however valuable that may have been in general terms: 'One thing that we always had thrown at us at college is that it's experience that counts, and I think you'll find at Geevor that experience tends to count far more than qualifications really. In fact the present mine superintendant isn't qualified, but he's been here more than thirty years, and he knows everybody in the mine.'

Jeremy's prospects for promotion are good, but he shares with the older hands like Edward Waters a more fundamental attachment to Geevor: 'You go up to Redruth and it's a totally different atmosphere. The guys there drive through tunnels sixteen feet square, and hardly ever get out of their trucks and actually get in contact with the rock. The only time they actually touch the rock is when they are charging up for blasting. Redruth – as far as I am concerned – is an underground quarry, whereas down here you actually feel you are in the middle of it. Geevor is the smallest of the lot, but I think you will find it is the happiest place to work.'

Even in the hardest times St Just miners were probably better off than the rest of the community, and that edge of élitism is still maintained by wage rates slightly higher than average for the area. Jeremy gave us an outline: 'The basic underground labourer earns about £75 a week, and he can usually make an extra £13 on top of that for a Saturday morning. A trammer can pick up £90–£100 a week, and the machine-men, the drillers, in the region of £150–£200 a week. Mind you, they don't earn that by sitting around drinking tea all day, but they work in pairs and they don't have to kill themselves these days to make good money. The real high-flyers are getting a lot more than that. They are the developers who are paid by how much ground they break, so much per metre advanced as they extend the levels. As far as safety goes, there are certain domestic regulations and as long as you stick to them there should be no problem, but basically each man looks to his own safety. You check your working base every day. In some places there is more bad ground than others, depending on the lie of the lode. These narrow lodes can vary considerably in width, dip and tin content.' For all the modern aids, today's miner at Geevor still needs all his ancestors' awareness of his surroundings.

Even with his experience so far Jeremy Green could no doubt easily take off with his wife and see the world, acquiring the itchy feet that many Cornishmen originally developed through sheer necessity. It seems more likely though, that with the promise of an assured future at home, they will choose the simpler contentment of their roots. Possibly too in thirty years' time they will be walking the cliffs at Botallack echoing the same sentiments as Laura Rowe: 'In our row now we've got Cornish people in every house except one. So that's nice, it's friendly and comfortable. It may be a cowardly sort of thing to want that kind of security around you, but I think what *we* had was security and we want to keep that for our children. Mind you, there are people who come down here that wouldn't dream of harming it. They think for the place, and they'll fight for it. But then you get people who come down here just to exploit, and that's terrible. They bring more and more visitors and that sort of thing does harm. We're losing a lot of things that are going to be very precious soon, and I think that's sad . . .'

Then after a pause, Laura said: 'Perhaps my politics are a bit soft . . .'

Guiting Power

'It wasn't that I came along with high-falutin' ideas about what I was going to do with this village. It was the village, and its people, that got me . . .'

To the eighty per cent of us who are properly described as 'urban dwellers', taking a step into a Cotswold village like Guiting Power inevitably has the initial sensation of a step back in time. Around the green mound of 'The Square', an irregular cluster of yellow stone cottages sits tight; the few remaining stones of a market cross lie in the grass next to a modest war memorial bearing nineteen names from the First World War, but none from the Second; and the air is tinged with the smell of new-baked bread from the village bakery on the corner.

But any impression that this village is a charming museum piece, ticking over in its nineteenth-century state to please the visitor's eye, soon evaporates. Along the lane the village school buzzes with the activities of two classes of primary-age children, while in the village hall beyond a couple of dozen pre-school toddlers yell their way through a morning of paint and play. Taking a ploughman's lunch in 'The Farmers' Arms' may well mean rubbing shoulders with a real ploughman in for his midday pint of cider, and later in the afternoon when the school bus is back from Bourton-on-the-Water, the bells of St Michael's parish church might be heard as a group of the village teenagers get to grips with a peal that has been neglected for years. Back in 'The Farmers'' the young men of the tug o' war team, off to practise, come in with a two-gallon can for cider, and later in the evening this community pub really comes to life with some combination of darts, skittles, air-gun shooting, pool, quoits and 'Country and Western' all going on in their appropriate corners on their respective nights. The visitor too is as welcome to join in as the locals.

This lively and confident village atmosphere is by no means an accident. Since 1958 about half the houses and over one thousand acres of farmland around it have been the domain of one man, Raymond Cochrane. He lives in a large house which he restored on

The Manor House, formerly Woodhouse, home of George East's grandfather

the western fringes of the parish, and from there exerts a degree of benevolent despotism over the environment of fifty per cent of the inhabitants, and by implication therefore over the rest as well. But it was not a responsibility he was seeking when he first looked at Guiting Power. For twenty-five years Mr Cochrane had farmed in Wiltshire. Originally a Scot and educated as an academic, he had inherited a substantial amount of money through his mother at the age of twenty-one. Then a love of the English countryside and recurrence of childhood tuberculosis made him stumble into farming. In the 1950s he was looking for additional land, principally to solve an animal feeding problem. His attention was drawn to an advertisement by Tippett & Taylor, Chartered Auctioneers and Estate Agents of Bourton-on-the-Water for:

> an attractive freehold, residential and excellent sporting property and important agricultural investment on the borders of the Cotswold,

Decay and dereliction – typical of Guiting Power cottages before 1958

North Cotswolds and Heythrop Hunts, at Guiting Power, one of the very attractive small Cotswold villages, which lies in the upper valley of the River Windrush in a district well-known for its social and sporting amenities.

With the estate went the role of Lord of the Manor. It included the Manor House, three farms, thirty-three cottages and various other houses, buildings and properties. The advertisement had referred to cottages 'in need of modernisation and improvement'; in fact most were semi-dilapidated, and eighteen were 'condemned' by the local authority. Mr Cochrane was not at all interested in the sporting amenities, but says he was much concerned at the near-slum conditions in which many Guiting Power tenants were living, and horrified by the prospect of a Cotswold village virtually disintegrating through neglect.

His first reaction was to avoid the responsibility. But he found:

'Guiting Power involved so much more than a farming proposition . . . I'd always been very much interested in domestic architecture, I'd come to love the Cotswolds when an undergraduate at Oxford, and, above all, Guiting was a challenge. It is not an "architectural gem", since most of its present houses were built or re-built at the beginning of the nineteenth century in what one might call Regency vernacular – a very plain style. But the lay-out is most attractive and dates from at least medieval times . . . though not "pretty", it has excellent structure.

'It seemed to me that the village itself – the houses – was desperately asking for help. I had inherited some money . . . to what better use could I put this surplus than to restore and internally modernise these houses for the benefit of local people, who had put up with so much for so long? The estate, sold at the then going rate, cost less than £60,000. It was to cost about five times that amount to put it in order, which represented most of my assets.'

The Guiting Manor Trust was formed at once. It is a charitable trust, which then included some three dozen houses and plots of land in the village 'to ensure their conservation in perpetuity'. Mr Cochrane explained that it was the only way in which restoration work on such a scale could be considered. The agricultural rents too were brought into play in 1974 when Guiting Manor Farms became a tenant of the Trust.

Mr Cochrane is anxious to dispel any ideas that he is behaving like a feudal Lord of the Manor: 'It wasn't that I came along with high-falutin' ideas about what *I* was going to do with this village. It was the village, and its people, that got *me*. I'm really a very unsuitable person for this job because I'm a loner, and rather unsociable. But my wife helped a lot.'

Guiting Power's history goes back to the Stone Age, but for most of the time it has been a poor hill village. It had bursts of prosperity – in 1330 it acquired a market licence, and in the fifteenth century enjoyed the wool boom as did the rest of the Cotswolds. The land was enclosed in 1798, and in the Napoleonic Wars, with farming – and later quarrying – doing well, was again reasonably prosperous. The population reached its peak of eight hundred in 1831, but after 1850 declined steadily. The combination of a series of absentee or unconcerned landlords, depressions in agriculture and industrial expansion elsewhere, seems to have sucked the life from Guiting Power, as it did from many English villages. In 1958 there were less than three hundred inhabitants.

Mr Cochrane set out to restore the life of the village to something nearer its heyday, not so much by turning the clock back, but by attempting to 'blend the aesthetic with the practical', by making the village a convenient and attractive place for its own community to live in. Housing at economic rents was placed within reach of local young couples and, as far as it lay within Mr Cochrane's power, wealthy weekenders from the Midlands were not encouraged. He saw the charitable trust as the first essential tool in the campaign:

'It may be more blessed to give than receive, but it's a damn sight more difficult. But it's the only way you can keep things together because of Capital Transfer Tax and so on. Even if I'd had a son or sons to carry on, on the one hand they probably wouldn't have been able to afford to, and on the other you can never be sure your successor will have similar ideas. So now I work as Steward for my own Trust. Of course I don't take anything for it, because it's absolutely essential that an original owner doesn't benefit personally from a charitable trust.'

Events moved rapidly in the next six years. By 1964 he was able to report:

'. . . forty-two houses have been restored and modernised, four others have been re-roofed, and two considerably altered. Only three have not been modernised, because their elderly tenants do not wish to be disturbed . . . The old smithy has been made into a bus shelter . . . the bakery has been moved and modernised, and a workshop made from a derelict house . . . A new village hall-cum-sports pavilion has been built. Three old stone barns have been restored and five sets of modern farm buildings erected. Thirty-four stone roofs have been re-laid . . . and fourteen garages erected.'

The restoration of buildings was carried out in accordance with Mr Cochrane's almost fanatical eye for architectural detail. Doorways, windows, gutters, chimney stacks, even door panels, all were modified for period and scale. Buildings beyond repair were demolished and the materials used elsewhere, and one of the larger buildings, Greenfield House, lost its third storey to retrieve its proper Georgian proportions. Only a few slate roofs were left because of the prohibitive cost of replacing all of them with the original stone.

Despite the building work the people of Guiting Power were not

The old smithy, now a bus shelter

overlooked. Elderly tenants were left undisturbed without modern conveniences if they preferred it, but positive steps were taken to add to the community's meagre amenities. The local council was persuaded to install mains drainage. A village hall was built to replace the old timber and asbestos 'concert hall', and then handed over, rent-free, to a management committee to run on behalf of the village. Now hardly a day passes, summer or winter, without at least one group using its facilities.

The ploughing back of the Trust's income into the community has also allowed Mr Cochrane to practise a degree of what might be called 'social husbandry'. The former stables of Greenfield House are being converted into a series of flatlets for elderly people with the object of releasing a number of two- or three-bedroom cottages for local young couples with families. Once again, the elderly are not being uprooted against their wish, but gentle persuasion is being used in order to increase the prospects of the next generation remaining in the village.

There can be no doubt of Mr Cochrane's benevolent intentions. He is following through a policy that could benefit many threatened country communities:

'We tried to stimulate a real rural community, and give all the encouragement we could to local people who were being gradually priced out of their village. These days they can't afford the price that the merest cottage fetches. There's a terrible danger – and it's already happened in many Cotswold villages – that they're swamped by outsiders. Then they lose their character, they become 'suburbanised' by town dwellers coming into the country, whereas I think we should remain as we are, a rural-oriented community.'

The aims for this tiny Cotswold Utopia are obviously laudable, and the work of the last twenty-two years has certainly transformed the village into a very desirable place to live. The house waiting list was closed to outsiders ten years ago, as the Trust is determined that Guiting shall be one English village where the native-born population gets preferential treatment. But it does occur to the onlooker to wonder whether one man's grand design can survive the attacks of human nature.

As landlord of 'The Farmers' Arms', Tony Miles might be said to sit at the hub of village life. The Miles family have been in the village for generations, his grandfather had his own bus and wagon business and his cousin still runs the village garage. His parents held the pub licence until his father died, although his mother, Vera, still presides behind the bar on occasion. Although like all landlords he never repeats exactly what he hears, Tony's daily exposure to village news and views, as well as a long spell as a parish councillor, have left him well-placed to assess the changes:

'Whereas the estates in the old days probably employed fifty or sixty, nowadays a two-thousand-acre estate can be farmed with about five or six men, so youngsters are finding it more and more difficult. But there again with most people having cars, they just travel on into Cheltenham or somewhere like that and find jobs in factories. Our present landowners are making sure that houses are available to young married couples. They've no problem finding a house if they are local people, so they have encouraged them to stay. It's just the work problem really. So long as they can find work, they can always find a house. I think the general view is that Mr Cochrane has done a tremendous lot for the village since he's been here. With one or two things, of course, he rubs people up the wrong way, but I suppose that's only natural, isn't it?'

The Trust's monthly newsheet, *The Guiting Gazette*, written by

A house on the square, before restoration

Mr Cochrane, has occasionally proved a source of such irritations, apart from a literary style which distinguishes its writer from most of its readers, but, as Tony Miles explained, there is little surprise in most quarters if their Lord of the Manor occasionally behaves in a high-handed, almost aristocratic manner. In fact it seems to be almost expected. 'I think that's what most village squires are like. They're a bit above the peasants, as you might call it, but most village people will accept that anyway. He's the village squire, and that's it. He's not unreasonable, by any means. Anybody with a problem can contact him any time, and he'll see them. Nobody in his position nowadays thinks he's the sort of village squire that can ride about on his charger and you have to bow down your head as he goes past!'

Among Tony Miles's regulars at 'The Farmers' Arms' are George and Connie East, who refer to Mr Cochrane genially as 'the boss'. Both are members of the parochial church council and are busily involved in many of the village's activities. George, one of Guiting Manor Farm's workers, now one of its shareholders, this year brought

The same house, later, won a Civic Trust Award

in his forty-sixth harvest. He often recalls a harvest over twenty years ago when Mr Cochrane came out to George in the fields and, signalling to him to stop the combine, presented him with a five-pound note to open a savings account for his new-born son, the first child to be born on the estate since Mr Cochrane's arrival.

The Easts have farmed locally for quite a few generations. George's grandfather once lived as a tenant farmer in 'Woodhouse', now Mr Cochrane's home, and therefore called the 'Manor House'. The present generations of Easts live in one of the restored Trust cottages, but George well remembers the state of the village in 1958: 'It was pretty rough really. All the houses were getting into a pretty bad state of repair. I suppose there was a bit of resentment when Mr Cochrane started changing things, but he gave the land for a sewage set-up and that made all the difference. People had had to dig a hole in the garden, which wasn't very pleasant, so some of them got bathrooms for the first time.'

He also watched Mr Cochrane's policy stabilise the local popu-

George and Connie East. George, a veteran of forty-six harvests in Guiting, is now a shareholder in Guiting Manor Farms

lation: 'Some years earlier people from Birmingham had taken some of the cottages as week-end cottages. They were sort of well-to-do people compared with the country people, although some of the cottages, I remember in my time, were sold for about £70 each. I've seen people come back over the years, thinking they could do the same. But it won't happen again now.'

If the local people have for the most part been prepared to accommodate Mr Cochrane's ways, more vocal opposition has come at times from some of the owner-occupiers, many of them 'new residents' or 'people from Birmingham', the local generic description for former town-dwellers. A storm developed at the end of 1978 over permission granted by the Trust to an exploration company to drill for oil on their land. Most of the indigenous population were behind Mr Cochrane's closely-defined agreement to the operation, while the opposition came mainly from the newcomers, no doubt fearing the devastation of their chosen spot in rural England. The controversy

Tony Miles presides at 'The Farmers' Arms'

flared and died as the drillers came, found no oil and went away. They left nothing behind them but a few souvenir rock samples, and perhaps the feeling that the long-term stability of the Guiting Power community will depend on more than the purpose of Mr Cochrane and his successors.

It may be that the factors which made Mr Cochrane an 'outsider' in 1958 also gave him the detachment necessary for so bold a task as regenerating this small piece of rural England. He has few illusions about the toes he may have stepped on from time to time: 'The village people were very suspicious and rightly so. In fact they were terribly suspicious of the Trust. Because there wasn't an obvious financial benefit to be gained, they wondered what I was doing underneath. We did what needed to be done and gradually we developed, I think I can say, a very good relationship, especially with our local people. We come up against a few of the "outsider" residents who want to shout at us for one thing or another, whether it's oil or anything else. But, for example, I've been trying hard of recent years to bring the council house people into the picture. We don't want our tenants to be a privileged lot in the village, and the council house people out on a limb. Now we interchange. People go from us to them sometimes, if they want a bigger house, and we're probably going to take some of their tenants into our smaller houses. So the suspicions have gradually worn out.'

One occasional source of friction with the tenants themselves would appear to be the rules and restrictions applied by the Trust in the name of conservation. It is a policy that may have won Guiting Power the Best Kept Village award in 1964, but to some the restrictions obviously seem petty and excessive. To Mr Cochrane it is a simple matter: 'We have an informal agreement with our tenants and if they make a mess of the garden, or stick up a caravan, or something like that, then we come down quite heavily. After all we are a Conservation Area, and we really play on the pride that people have in the village.'

We wondered if this constant watch might inhibit the Trust house tenants from voicing any criticism of their landlord, but Mr Cochrane doubted it: 'I don't notice any great fear about. Oh no, I think what has happened is what I hoped would happen – we work on a basis of mutual respect. We respect them immensely, and I think they've come to respect us. Perhaps it's a hang-back to the fourteenth century when they had their own market, but Guiting people are still very independent – and I respect them for that even when they go for me.'

Most people in Guiting Power, including Mr Cochrane, show concern in planning the future for the village children. George and Connie East, for example, have five children growing up. Michael, the eldest, is already in the army and away in Germany, their daughter Anita is at technical college, and Rachel and the twins Clare and Andrew are still at school in Bourton-on-the-Water.

Connie is quite realistic about their chances locally: 'Andrew wants to go into farming, and he'll probably find a living round here, but the others, I'm afraid, will have to go out of the village. I think children know what they want to do these days, and they have the opportunities, like going to college. They make up their minds what they're going to do and even if those things were in the village, I don't think they'd stay unless they wanted to.'

Though at present the girls enjoy village life, the chances are that they will move away, as so many more options are open to them now than the choice of marrying a local lad or going into service in the big houses. The boys have already made their choice, and George seemed satisfied: 'Michael always wanted to go into the army, that was his choice and we never tried to stop him. Andrew will be hired eventually, I think. There'll always be something to do on these farms – somebody's got to do the work, haven't they?'

He laughed, but Connie perhaps felt he was being over-modest on her son's behalf, so she added: 'They always used to say the village idiot went on the farms, but you can't be an idiot today with these machines. They terrify me at times.'

One constant topic of village conversation, especially among those with younger children, is the survival of the village school. Its retention is a matter of urgency both to the villagers and to the Trust. In George East's day there were a hundred and one pupils of all ages crammed into the small school building near the church, but at present there are only eighteen children of primary age divided into two classes. The village has won a stay of execution on the school for two years and on present estimates of over thirty children before that time is up, they are hopeful of securing the school's future for some years to come.

Besides a fifteen-year-old daughter, Tony Miles has a daughter who has just moved on to secondary school in Bourton, and a young son, Richard, who is one of those soon to make up the numbers in the village school. He stressed the problems that many villages with school closures face: 'The school is quite an important part of the life of the village. Besides, if the children have to go elsewhere it means buses, and for youngsters of five years old, they've got to leave at eight o'clock in the morning and they're not home again until quarter past four. It's a long day for five-year-old children. Also, they get a lot more individual attention in a small school. In the school at Bourton for instance, with larger classes, there's no doubt about it, the teachers just haven't got the time to look after children individually.'

Community consciousness too begins in school. When we visited the two classes, Miss Scott, surely everyone's ideal as a village school head, was helping the junior group make a model of the village. All the children, as well as the teacher, who lives in the village, already knew the name of every cottage's occupants. With the infants too it was

Miss Scott, *right*, working with one of her pupils in the village school

particularly warming, on a thin March morning, to see the chilly free milk turned into steaming mugs of cocoa.

To Mr Cochrane the school is integral to his aims for the village: 'If you don't have a school, you don't get the community feel at all. There have been threats to our school because from a bulge of forty-eight pupils we went rattling down to under twenty. So we were a bit scared of what might happen. But the Trust policy has been to give priority to local young couples and that is where we can score. You see, if houses are sold, they go to outsiders, mostly retired people, or people whose children have grown up, and who probably wouldn't send their children to the school if they had any. But we've been able to provide houses for fourteen young couples in the last few years.'

While the whole village undoubtedly sees the value of its school to the community, even in this area there are shades of opinion that differ from Mr Cochrane's. His delighted comments in the pages of *The Guiting Gazette* about the number of pregnant wives in the village caused some raised eyebrows. Some of the young mothers and mothers-to-be were slightly offended at the suggestion that they were doing their bit for the village. One of them said: 'He makes us sound like breeding cattle!' In this case perhaps it was merely a matter of tone.

While Mr Cochrane's faith in the principle of mutual respect is not misplaced as far as local people are concerned, there are those among them to whom the workings of the Trust seem more mysterious than they should. One of these is Bernard Saunders, one of the young men housed by the Trust, whose father has worked on the farm for Mr Cochrane from the beginning: 'Obviously there's been a vast improvement as far as the housing is concerned since Mr Cochrane took over and he has stopped a lot of modern-day eyesores being put up, but nobody knows enough about the Trust, and how it works. All we are told is a lot of rules and that's the end of it. One thing I'd like to know is what's going to happen when Mr Cochrane's gone, because there's nobody that actually represents the village on the Trust. There's nobody that's lived in the village most of their lives to speak for us – we have to rely on total outsiders.'

In fact one of the trustees does now live in the village and is deeply involved in community life. The others are by profession a solicitor and an accountant and, until his death in 1979 an architect, for whom a replacement is being sought, all of whose skills are no doubt needed to run the complex business of the Trust.

But apart from his feelings about outsiders, Bernard Saunders sees another problem as much more fundamental. He runs a vehicle repair business in buildings on the fringe of a quarry two miles out of the village: 'Work is the biggest problem really. We've had problems fighting for planning just for the garage here. There was a building here that had stood longer than I've been alive, and yet just because we wanted to change its use, we had a great deal of trouble with the planning people. Yet we employ as many people here in the garage as Guiting Manor Farm does.'

Bernard's disagreement on the subject of work is as much with the planning authorities as it is with the Trust, but after falling foul of the Trust at home over what he saw as over-zealous restrictions in the

Barley harvest at Guiting Manor Farm 1980: Arthur Harding, farm manager, *centre* with some of the workers

name of conservation, he decided to move out of the village: 'Over all, I can't quite understand their idea of conservation, and what they're trying to conserve. If you can't put buildings up, how are you going to bring work? They don't like cars and lorries and so on going through the village. Well, fair enough, but it's work, isn't it? It's all very well seeing it as a nice, pretty little village, but life has to go on somehow. To be able to live there you've got to be able to work.'

To be fair to the Trustees, they are not unaware of the problem. The Trust already employs five full-time building workers, some of whom have moved into Guiting from other Cotswold villages, like Eric Sharratt, the building foreman, who has been with the Trust for nearly twenty years. The Trustees also want to encourage further 'discreet industry', but the limitations imposed by their primary purpose of conservation inevitably result in not going as far or as fast as some local people would like. Even their own carefully laid plans for light industry have come up against the planning authority because of the site they chose.

One local proposal at least had received a favourable hearing. As Mr Cochrane reported to a meeting of the Trustees:

'Two young men who are qualified engineers are very anxious to start up a small engineering business of their own. I told them I thought you would agree to putting up a small workshop for them provided we could get the necessary planning permission. We've thought about a site which is on the village side of our grain storage and estate workshop where we've already planted a lot of chestnut trees to screen the buildings. These two chaps would start on their own but would hope in time to expand a bit and give employment to something up to ten people, most of whom we hope would be local people. Even our most preservation-minded residents seem to think that this is desirable . . .'

This last was obviously a reference to the 'anti-oil lobby'. Mr Cochrane is firmly in the camp that believes it is not enough to win best-kept village awards, to have a thriving school or a constant stream of activities in the village hall. He was horrified too at the suggestion that the village might be seen as a memorial to him when he goes: 'All we're concerned to do is to provide the means for people to fulfil themselves, for the village to fulfil itself. I can't predict, nor should I, where it will go. It's not for me to say – it's an open-ended business. I just hope we can provide the background. I've sometimes felt I was dragging Guiting backwards through a hedge into the twentieth century, but of course it's changed an awful lot in the last twenty-two years. The standard of living has improved immensely, which I am delighted to see.'

There can be no avoiding the conclusion that this bit of rural England owes its present vitality to a landowner who, in search of more land, took on a village as well. As he says, modestly enough: 'As far as I can make out, no Lord of the Manor has ever lived here and cared for Guiting, rather than making a profit from it.'

At first it sounds unlikely, but then if one remembers how manors have been bought and sold, used and abused down the centuries, he may well be right.

Acknowledgments

Acknowledgment is due to the following for permission to reproduce photographs:

AEROFILMS Hull docks, page 93; ASHINGTON ASSOCIATION FOOTBALL CLUB team, page 61; THE ASHINGTON GROUP paintings, page 66, and colour nos. 3 & 4; BARNABY'S PICTURE LIBRARY Whitby harbour (W. F. Meadows), page 76, sheep (Mustograph), page 136, Hull docks (van der Vaeren), colour no. 6; BBC HULTON PICTURE LIBRARY shipwreck, page 77, Hull, page 92, unloading timber, page 98; BRITISH TOURIST AUTHORITY Whitby harbour, colour no. 5, Kersey, colour no. 8; BRITISH TRANSPORT DOCKS BOARD unloading bananas, page 103, G. A. Cullington, page 107; CAMBRIDGE EVENING NEWS bumps race, page 109, college, page 110; DENNIS CARTWRIGHT college feast, colour no. 7; DAVID CLARKE wrestling, page 175; DUDLEY METROPOLITAN BOROUGH COUNCIL coal mine, page 12, chain shop, page 13, Dudley, colour no. 1; EAST LONDON ADVERTISER (Tony Furby) Cohen's shop, page 139, Kelly's shop, page 142; HEART OF ENGLAND TOURIST BOARD inn, page 19; HMS OSPREY, PORTLAND (Crown Copyright) naval base, page 158; HULL DAILY MAIL the Pen, page 95, W. Cunningham, page 107; INSTITUTE OF GEOLOGICAL SCIENCES (NERC copyright) tin mine, page 173; LANCASHIRE EVENING POST Hoghton Tower: gatehouse, page 45, hall, page 49, courtyard, page 50; LONDON BOROUGH OF TOWER HAMLETS, CENTRAL LIBRARY Cohen's shop, page 148; MANSELL COLLECTION Turner engraving, page 10; JOHN MILLER viaduct, page 30, West Sampson Hall, page 126, Manor Farm, page 132, tied cottages, page 133, John Comben, page 167, cricket, colour no. 2, church, colour no. 9; NATIONAL COAL BOARD, NORTH EAST miners, page 70, colliery, page 71; NORTHUMBERLAND COUNTY COUNCIL, ASHINGTON COUNTY LIBRARY Ashington, page 59; NORTHUMBERLAND GAZETTE football, page 69; OLDHAM EVENING CHRONICLE Uppermill, page 26, Delph, page 27, rushcart, pages 40 & 41; R. G. W. PHILLIPS dogs, page 23; RADIO TIMES museum (Don Smith), page 15, mill (Warwick Bedford), page 34, Sir Bernard (George Crane), both page 57, miners' picnic (Barry Wilkinson), page 72, fishermen (George Crane), pages 84 & 89, docks (Barry Wilkinson), pages 102 & 104, Harry Littlechild (Chris Ridley), page 112, college staff (Chris Ridley), pages 113 & 117, Partridge family (Don Smith), pages 125 & 131, Roman Road stallholders (Chris Ridley), pages 143, 144, 146, 150 & 153, 'Skylark' Durston (Don Smith), page 161, Edward Waters (Chris Ridley), page 178, Jeremy Green (Chris Ridley), page 186, the Easts (Chris Ridley), page 198, harvesting (Chris Ridley), page 204, quarrymen (Don Smith), colour no. 10; the Rowes (Chris Ridley), colour no. 12; LAURA ROWE painting, colour no. 11; SPECTRUM post office, colour no, 13; THE SUTCLIFFE GALLERY fishing boats, page 78, 'Morning & Evening', page 79; THOMAS WILLIAMS (LONGBOROUGH) LTD derelict houses, pages 191 & 196; DAVID & JOAN WILLS miners, page 177.

The photographs of Guiting Power on pages 190, 194, 197, 199 and 202 were taken for the BBC by the Butt Studio; and those of Portland on pages 157 & 168 by Reg Vincent.

Bibliography

General
CHALKLIN, C. W. and HAVINDEN, M. A. *Rural change and urban growth, 1500–1800* Longman, 1974.
CLARK, P. and SLACK, P. *Crisis and order in English towns, 1500–1700* Routledge and Kegan Paul, 1972.
COBBETT, W. *Rural Rides* 1830. Macdonald, Facsim. of 1830 edn. 1975; Penguin Books, 1967.
DEFOE, D. *A tour thro' the whole Island of Great Britain* 1724–27. (Everyman) Dent, 1975; Penguin Books, 1971.
FINBERG, H. P. R. *The agrarian history of England and Wales* vol. 4. *1500–1640* ed. by J. Thirsk. Cambridge University Press, 1967.
FRANKENBERG, R. *Communities in Britain* Penguin Books, 1970.
MORRIS, C. ed. *The journeys of Celia Fiennes* Cresset Press, 1947.
PRIESTLEY, J. B. *English Journey* Heinemann, 1934; Penguin Books 1977.

The Black Country
BIRD, V. *Bird's eye view of the Midlands* Roundwood Press, 1973.
BURRITT, E. *Walks in the Black Country and its green borderland* 1868. Roundwood Press, n.e. 1976.
CHANDLER, G. and HANNAH, I. C. *Dudley: as it was and as it is today* Batsford, 1949.
HILLIER, C. *The West Midlands: a journey to the heart of England* Gollancz, 1976; Paladin, 1978.
RAVEN, J. *The urban and industrial songs of the Black Country and Birmingham* Wolverhampton: Broadside Records, 1977.
RAVEN, J. *The folklore of Staffordshire* Batsford, 1978.

Saddleworth
TURNER, G. *The north country* Eyre and Spottiswoode, 1967.

Hoghton
BIRTILL, G. *In the footsteps of the faithful: a history of St Joseph's Brindle, 1677–1977* Brindle, Chorley: St Joseph's, 1979.
MILLER, G. C. *Hoghton Tower: the history of the manor, the hereditary lords and the ancient manor house of Hoghton in Lancashire* Preston: Guardian Press, 1948.

Ashington
FRASER, G. M. *The Steel Bonnets: the story of the Anglo–Scottish border reivers* Barrie and Jenkins, 1971; Pan, 1974.
NEWTON, R. *The Northumberland landscape* (Making of the English landscape) Hodder and Stoughton, 1972.

Whitby
GASKIN, R. T. *The old seaport of Whitby* Whitby: Forth/John Hudson, 1909.
HUMBLE, A. F. *Prints of old Whitby* Whitby: Literary and Philosophical Society, 1972.
HUMBLE, A. F. *The rowing lifeboats of Whitby* Whitby: Horne, 1974.
SHAW JEFFREY, P. *Whitby, lore and legend* Whitby: Horne, 1951.

Dockland, Hull
TURNER, G. *The north country* Eyre and Spottiswoode, 1967.
TURNER, T. *Diary of the docks dispute, 1972–3* University of Hull, Industrial Studies Unit, 1980.

Sidney Sussex College, Cambridge
SCOTT-GILES, C. W. *Sidney Sussex College: a short history* Cambridge University Press, 1975.

Kersey
EVANS, G. E. *The horse in the furrow* Faber, 1967. (and other titles)
FINCHAM, P. *The Suffolk we live in* George Nobbs Publishing, 1976.
SCARFE, N. *Suffolk* (Making of the English landscape) Hodder and Stoughton, 1972.

Roman Road, Bow
MAYHEW, H. *London labour and the London poor* 1861–2. (Victorian times) F. Cass, 4 vols. 1967; Dover Pubs., 4 vols. paperback 1969.

Portland
BETTEY, J. H. *The Island and Royal Manor of Portland* University of Bristol, Dept. of Extra Mural Studies, 1970.
BETTEY, J. H. *'The supply of stone for rebuilding St Paul's Cathedral'* in *Archaeological Journal* vol. 128, 1972. pp 176–85.

St Just-in-Penwith
HALLIDAY, F. E. *A history of Cornwall* Duckworth, n.e. paperback 1976.
RUHRMUND, F. *About St Just in Penwith* Bodmin: Bossiney Books, 1979.

Guiting Power
FINBERG, J. *The Cotswolds* Eyre Methuen, 1977.
HADFIELD, C. and A. *The Cotswolds: a new study* David and Charles, 1973.